12.99

D0120008

starting
your
business

DK small business *guides*

starting
your
business

PETER HINGSTON

A Dorling Kindersley Book

Dorling **DK** Kindersley

LONDON, NEW YORK, SYDNEY, DELHI, PARIS,
MUNICH, and JOHANNESBURG,

Senior Art Editor Jamie Hanson
DTP Designer Julian Dams
Production Controller Michelle Thomas

Managing Editor Adèle Hayward
Senior Managing Editor Stephanie Jackson
Senior Managing Art Editor Nigel Duffield

Produced for Dorling Kindersley by
Grant Laing Partnership
48 Brockwell Park Gardens,
London SE24 9BJ

Managing Editor Jane Laing
Project Editor Jane Simmonds
Project Art Editor Christine Lacey
Picture Researcher Jo Walton

First published in Great Britain in 2001
by Dorling Kindersley Limited,
9 Henrietta Street, London WC2E 8PS

2 4 6 8 10 9 7 5 3 1

A CIP catalogue record for this book is available from the British
Library

ISBN 0 7513 1413 7

Colour reproduction in Italy by GRB Editrice
Printed and bound by Mondadori in Verona, Italy

see our complete catalogue at
www.dk.com

CONTENTS

INTRODUCTION

Starting your own business is a huge step to take, and is likely to herald a major change in the direction of your life. This book is a comprehensive and, above all, practical guide to planning, starting, and running your own business.

A large part of the process is learning the hard way; *Starting Your Business* will prepare you for some of the possible pitfalls ahead. But becoming an entrepreneur can also be fun: you will learn a broad range of skills and deal with people and situations you have never encountered before. Finally, starting and running a successful business can be a uniquely fulfilling experience: you may be putting your dreams into action, providing employment for others, and creating a life for yourself where you make the decisions.

This book takes you through the process – from getting to know how your own skills and abilities equip you for running your business, and developing your initial business idea, to making your plans more concrete and raising the money you will need.

Finding premises and staff are covered, along with ways of selling and marketing, both at home and abroad. Financial aspects of running your business are discussed in detail, including day-to-day accounts and dealing with financial problems. Long-term plans are also dealt with – whether you want your business to keep expanding into new areas or simply to provide a means for your retirement. The final section of the book is an up-to-date guide to all the legal and financial matters likely to affect you as a small business. There are suggestions for useful contacts and further reading, plus a glossary.

Starting Your Business is suitable for the self-employed (sole traders), partnerships, and limited companies, and for all types of business, including builders, caterers, consultants, designers, exporters, garages, hotel owners, internet firms, manufacturers, office services, and retailers. Time is precious when you are starting in business: this book can be read from cover to cover, or you can dip into the relevant sections as you need to. Due to the many complexities involved when starting or running a business, you would benefit from taking sound professional advice before making any important decisions.

BEFORE you start

Some of the most important decisions concerning your new business need to be made long before you have your first customer. The key to building a sound, viable business is to combine thorough research with careful, detailed planning, covering every aspect of the business – from developing your initial idea, to finding the finance, to locating new premises.

DOING THE GROUNDWORK

Starting your own business, be it a modest part-time undertaking or a major enterprise, can be one of life's important milestones. Before you set out on such a great adventure, it is important to establish whether starting a business is likely to be the right step for you. Being your own boss, and maybe that of other people, does not suit everybody, but if it suits you, you are unlikely to want to work for anyone else again. This chapter includes three self-assessments to help you understand your motivation, your personal attributes, and your business skills and knowledge.

Most people's life experiences do not equip them fully to understand the implications of being self-employed. The main exceptions are those people born into families that run their own businesses and, to some degree, those who have been involved in sales. Working in a large organization gives you little idea of what it will be like to be your own boss, and working in the public sector helps even less. Starting your own business is not like changing your job – the differences are more profound and far-reaching. It is vital, therefore, to take the time to think about the reality and the consequences of starting your own business, and to assess and define exactly what you hope to achieve on a number of levels – including the personal, professional, and financial.

Be realistic about your strengths and weaknesses, and try to remedy the weaknesses

Ask yourself why you want to start your own business. Is it because you have always wanted to be your own boss? Is it because a friend suggested it? Is it because you are unhappy in your current job? Do you feel that you have something to prove? Whatever the reason for wanting to start your own business, be completely honest with yourself because, once you have set the wheels in motion, it will become increasingly difficult to back out without loss of capital, loss of face, and possibly the loss of any paid employment.

Having clear aims and ambitions that you are keen to fulfil is a great first step on the road to starting your own business. Work through the questions in the self-assessment exercise opposite to explore and analyze your own personal aims and motivations further.

CASE STUDY: Making the Most of Experience

ALISON WAS MADE redundant after the branch of the high-street bank where she was employed closed down. She enjoyed working on her own and found the idea of being her own boss very appealing; starting a business with her redundancy settlement seemed a natural option. In her banking work, Alison had been involved in introducing internet banking for customers and latterly had been responsible for liaising with the branch's business clients. As she enjoyed these aspects of her work, she decided to set up as a business consultant specializing in e-commerce. She could operate from home, and the low start-up costs and flexibility suited her. Although her existing skills and knowledge formed a good starting point, she signed up for a course in selling to brush up her sales technique.

ASSESSING YOUR AIMS

Completing this questionnaire will help you to determine whether starting your own business is the right move for you. It is not a test that you either pass or fail; the questions instead prompt you to assess your life aims. Take your time thinking about each one before answering "Yes" or "No", then read the comment that follows. By the end of the questionnaire, you should have a clearer idea of what motivates you, and how this equips you to run your own business.

Have you always wanted to run your own business? ☐Y ☐N

Having a long-held ambition to run your own business will help you get through difficult patches, and you are more likely to succeed in the end.

Do you know what work you would like to be doing in five or ten years? ☐Y ☐N

You need to take a long-term view, as it will take several years for the business to become established.

Do you want to work on your own? ☐Y ☐N

Starting a business can be a lonely experience, and it does not suit everyone. There tends to be less social contact than when working as an employee.

Do you want to be the boss? ☐Y ☐N

You will probably answer "Yes" to this question, but have you ever held a position of responsibility in a business or a club? Might you be happier working as a team member?

Is a career of less importance to you than other ambitions? ☐Y ☐N

If you are career-orientated, then self-employment is probably not for you.

Do you want to realize your full potential? ☐Y ☐N

Self-employment requires far more skills than many people realize. It will stretch you to the full, as you will probably have to do all the work associated with your business, especially in the early years.

Do you think you will have a better quality of life running your own business? ☐Y ☐N

Although you will undoubtedly work longer hours, particularly at the outset, most self-employed people feel their quality of life improves.

Do you expect to earn a lot of money? ☐Y ☐N

You will probably answer "Yes" to this question. Although some people start a business with the sole intention of making money, most seek independence and a better quality of life. This is just as well, since it usually takes several lean years of trading before a successful business becomes established and adequately profitable.

Would you like a greater degree of financial security? ☐Y ☐N

Although you will probably answer "Yes" to this question, you may believe that being self-employed will give you less financial security. At first this is usually the case but, in the long term, it is possible that you will have more security working for yourself as you have greater control over your own destiny.

Do you have a specific business idea you would like to see become a reality? ☐Y ☐N

Some people just want "to start a business", while others want to see their pet idea – a new product or business concept – become a reality. Experience shows the latter tend to be more motivated and likely to succeed.

RESULTS

If most of your answers to this questionnaire are "Yes", then it is a good indicator that starting a business might be the right step for you. If the majority of your answers are "No", think again about exactly what you hope to gain from starting your own business.

What is it Really Like?

Do you know what it is really like to own and run a small business? If not, take a methodical approach and find out as much as you can about the pros and cons. You may feel that you want to get started right away but, as any experienced entrepreneur will tell you, it is better to proceed with caution, taking small steps to avoid tripping up.

STUDYING EXISTING BUSINESSES

First, you could talk to anyone you know who is already self-employed. The best people to approach are family or friends, as they will take the time to talk to you, be candid about their own experiences, discuss your project, and give advice. Do not just focus on the good points – note and ask more about any downsides or cautions. Individual relatives or friends may even be prepared to act as mentors to guide you through the whole process.

Every day you will come into contact with people who run their own businesses, such as your local newsagent, plant nursery, taxi driver, hairdresser, and so on. They may not have time to sit and chat with you but are often happy to answer a few questions and generally give their opinions on self-employment. Later, note down what you learned from them. Bear in mind, though, that you may have to read between the lines: you are their customer, and they might feel they should provide a positive view, or want to give the impression that their business is a great success. They may even quote their turnover to you (if it is impressive), but they are likely to be more reticent about their actual profits, which are much more relevant to you.

To get a sense of what running your business might be like, try to visit a similar sort of establishment. This is easiest if you are thinking of starting a business with open access to the public, such as a shop, café, or small hotel. Walk in and look around. Look at the staff, the customers, the decor, and any stock. Can you imagine yourself running all this? If so, is there anything you would do differently? Would you enjoy the responsibility and the work on a daily basis? Try also to imagine the work that will be needed behind the scenes. If your proposed business is office-based or requires an industrial unit, it will be more difficult to experience. Some offices and industrial units may have open days or outer offices to which you can gain access, or you may be able to visit a friend who is employed in a similar workplace to get a feel for actually owning the business.

READING UP

Autobiographies or biographies of successful entrepreneurs can also provide valuable insights. Most started from nothing and ran small businesses to begin with, and it is revealing to learn which personal characteristics helped their businesses to survive and prosper. Many of their initial trials and mistakes are common to all businesses. Luck often plays a part, but is usually combined with qualities such as an ability to spot an opportunity, a dogged determination to succeed, and, in some cases, the use of clever or innovative ideas. Look at the assessment opposite to see which of the relevant attributes you possess.

LOOKING AT MISCONCEPTIONS

MYTH	REALITY
You will make lots of money.	Some do, some do not; most just manage.
You will have fewer work problems.	There will be a greater variety of problems – some serious.
You will have more spare time.	Most work longer hours and have fewer holidays than they would if they were not self-employed.

ASSESSING YOUR PERSONAL ATTRIBUTES

Read each of the following questions and then decide which of the answers best describes yourself. The questions are not in any order of importance. Score 4 points for each A answer, 2 points for each B answer, and 0 points for each C answer. Add up your scores, then look at the assessments in the Results panel at the bottom.

Are you able to concentrate?
- A I can concentrate on one thing for long periods. ☐
- B I am able to concentrate for some time. ☐
- C I am not too good at concentrating. ☐

Are you enthusiastic?
- A I get quite excited about things. ☐
- B I am guardedly enthusiastic. ☐
- C I rarely get excited about things. ☐

Are you a risk taker?
- A I like to minimize my risks. ☐
- B I am happy taking risks – personal or financial. ☐
- C I do not like taking any risks. ☐

Are you creative?
- A I enjoy thinking up new ideas. ☐
- B I find new things interesting. ☐
- C I do not think creativity is one of my attributes. ☐

Are you decisive?
- A I like to make decisions. ☐
- B I make decisions only if I have to. ☐
- C I hesitate because I am not sure what is right. ☐

Are you determined?
- A Once I start something, I like to see it through. ☐
- B I try hard but eventually stop if things are not working. ☐
- C I really cannot see the point of trying too hard. ☐

Are you good with figures?
- A I enjoy doing calculations, some without a calculator. ☐
- B I will work things out if I have to. ☐
- C I am not very confident with figures. ☐

Are you happy working long hours?
- A I am used to working evenings and some weekends. ☐
- B I do not mind working some evenings or weekends. ☐
- C I prefer not to work evenings or weekends. ☐

Are you self-confident?
- A I am happy to talk to new people in a business context. ☐
- B I have to force myself to approach new people. ☐
- C I do not really know – previously, I have rarely needed to approach new people. ☐

Are you well organized?
- A I usually have lists to work through and I set deadlines. ☐
- B I do not like to be disorganized. ☐
- C I sometimes forget to do things or I do them late. ☐

RESULTS

0–10 points
Are you really sure you are ready to run your own business? Think again about whether you are likely to be happy working for yourself.

12–20 points
You have strengths and weaknesses. You might consider involving someone else who has complementary attributes.

22–30 points
Although you have many attributes that make you suited to running your own business, you have a few weaknesses. Think about and improve upon the areas where you scored lowest.

32–40 points
Your personal attributes seem well suited to running your own business.

ECONOMIC CONSIDERATIONS

When considering what it is like to start your own business, an immediate and significant aspect is the economic one. When you start a business there is no regular pay cheque, and you will probably have to plunder your savings to fund the new venture. On the day you start up you may be rich in enthusiasm and ideas but, if you were previously in paid employment, you are likely to be poorer financially than you have been for a long time.

Make sure that your plans include an escape route

Ideally, where there are two people involved in starting a business, try to arrange matters so that one remains in relatively secure paid employment while the other works to set up the business. In this way there is continuing and predictable income to support domestic and other regular expenditure. At some future date the two people can decide when the new business is ready to support them both. This is a common start-up strategy. For more information on starting a new business as a sole trader, in a partnership, or as a limited company, see pp. 162–4.

INVOLVING OTHERS

As part of your pre-start preparations, you should discuss your ideas with all those who might be affected. This may not be relevant if you are single. If you have a partner and/or dependants, you need to discuss the ramifications of your decision to go it alone at some length and on several different occasions. They need to understand exactly what you are planning to do, the risks you will be taking, and how this could affect them should things get difficult. You need to assess whether you have their full support, which is vital. If your business is going to be home-based, either temporarily or permanently, this can introduce a whole new range of problems and strains. For more information about working from home, or choosing other premises, such as shops, offices, industrial units, or workshops, see pp. 68–75.

LIFESTYLE ASPECTS

A related issue is the lifestyle that you (and your family) are prepared to accept. This should be taken into account at a very early stage. Depending on the type of business you are intending to operate, your new lifestyle may involve financial anxiety and long or erratic working hours.

■ **SHOPS** These often have large stock, onerous leases (if rented), and may suffer from staffing problems. On the other hand, retail is a cash business – your customers do not expect any credit. Opening hours are set, but you have to be there to open up, whatever happens. Hours can also be very long – a small general store and newsagent demands a seven-day week with a very early start to the day, and possibly a late finish too. If you want to take a holiday, you may need either to close down while you are away or arrange for someone else to run the shop.

■ **MANUFACTURERS** These businesses may suffer from customers who take many months to pay (or never do). Some firms supply only one or two large companies and so are vulnerable if they lose a major customer, and most have to operate on small margins. However, at least you can close the door and go home on a Friday evening (even if you take some paperwork with you).

MONEY SAVER

Take advantage of the abundant free business advice that is available. It will help you to avoid at least some of the pitfalls of starting a new business, and in doing so will prevent you from losing your money (and wasting your time).

BALANCING WORK AND HOME LIFE

Whether you are working from home, or bringing work home, starting a small business is likely to have an impact on all aspects of your life, and demand large amounts of your time, at least until the venture is up and running.

■ **SERVICE BUSINESSES** Some have the advantages of requiring little stock and low overheads, and are quick to start up. These are also frequently the type of business that have fierce competition or are readily copied by competitors. Customers may expect the phone to be answered when they have a problem, even at 9 p.m. or at a weekend – or you may choose to offer this service to gain the edge over competitors.

These lifestyle aspects need full consideration, as they will be with you for the lifetime of your business. As your waking hours will be spent predominantly working at your new business, then you need to get it right. Once you have started a business you will be fully committed, and it is not easy to escape if you suddenly realize that you are unhappy and this is not what you had planned on doing.

THE APPEAL OF INDEPENDENCE

Everyone who starts a business thinks they will succeed but, in fact, around one in three will cease trading within a few years. Although some will give up without much distress, for others it will involve a great deal of pain and disillusionment. There is no sense in thinking "it will not happen to me": you should always plan a course of action for damage minimization should things not work out as hoped.

On the other hand, ask anyone who runs their own business if they made the right decision and their reply will usually be "yes". Many of those who fail try again at a later date. More surprisingly, even those people who work longer hours for less financial reward than they would have as an employee usually choose to remain their own boss. Many say it is the independence that self-employment provides that holds the essential appeal.

Business Skills and Knowledge

When you start your own business you need to have not only the right personal qualities, but also sufficient business skills and knowledge. Many people think that all they need is the technical or trade skills and experience to succeed in business but, in fact, it is probably more important to have general business skills and knowledge. Why is this the case? The reasons are many but experience has shown that small businesses thrive or fail principally due to general business reasons rather than the technical or trade skills of the proprietors. This assumes that your technical or trade abilities are at least adequate for your proposed business – only you will know if this is true. Although your skills are central to the success of your business, there is plenty of help at hand from other quarters, some in the form of free advice, and some from paid experts.

LEARNING NEW SKILLS
Before you start, and once your business is underway, take the time to update and supplement your knowledge by undertaking courses and training.

KEY SKILLS

Although a multitude of skills are needed to run a business, there are two that seem to lie at the core of business success:

- ■ **THE ABILITY TO SELL** Whether you are in a service, retail, or manufacturing business, this is essential. From the start you will need to sell your business and business plan to potential backers, and, once you are up and running, selling will bring in and maintain the revenues. Selling also incorporates negotiating skills, which are essential for giving you a financial edge, but also help generally in dealings with people.
- ■ **AN UNDERSTANDING OF MONEY** This has implications in all aspects of a business, from how to price your goods or services, to

recognizing a good deal from a bad one, and being able to keep the finances of the business in good shape.

The actual breadth and depth of knowledge required to survive in business is quite surprising to the uninitiated. Have a look at the self-assessment exercise opposite and test yourself to see how you rate. The good news about business knowledge is that it can be learned. Although a natural talent is an advantage, all of us can learn to do a good job if we are interested and motivated by the need to succeed in business. Many colleges provide training courses for small businesses, which are often run as evening classes. Subjects covered at these classes include bookkeeping, computer skills, marketing, and sales.

ASKING THE EXPERTS

In addition to strengthening your own skills, there are many other organizations and people you can call upon. These include:

- ■ **ACCOUNTANTS** Consult an accountant when setting up a business and to help with your tax returns. Accountants can help enormously with your business plan and in setting up good accounting systems. Choose carefully to find an accountant you are happy with who charges a reasonable fee.
- ■ **BANK MANAGERS** Banks have a good range of business knowledge and are keen to advise small businesses. Keep them abreast of any developments.
- ■ **BUSINESS DEVELOPMENT ORGANIZATIONS** Most of these organizations can answer your queries or put you in touch with the right person. Their advice is usually free.
- ■ **GOVERNMENT TAX OFFICES** Many of your straightforward tax queries can be answered by the appropriate tax office.
- ■ **LOCAL GOVERNMENT** They often have workshops and industrial units to rent and can advise on planning and licensing.
- ■ **SOLICITORS** Consult a solicitor before you start up, before you take over new premises, and for other legal queries.

Assessing Your Business Skills and Knowledge

Read each of the following questions and select the answer that best describes yourself. Score 4 points for each A answer, 2 points for each B answer, and 0 points for each C. Add up your scores, then read the Results panel at the bottom.

Do you understand your market?
A I have worked in this market for a long time. ☐
B I have some experience of this market. ☐
C I have no experience of this particular market. ☐

Do you know about marketing?
A I have a lot of experience of marketing, advertising, and so on. ☐
B I have some experience of marketing. ☐
C I do not really know about marketing. ☐

Do you have sales skills?
A I am an experienced sales professional. ☐
B I have done some selling in the past. ☐
C I have never sold anything before.* ☐
(Score 1 point if you have negotiated a good sale price for your own car.)*

Do you have experience dealing with customers?
A I have had to deal with customers for several years. ☐
B I have had to deal with customers on occasions. ☐
C I have never had to deal directly with customers. ☐

Do you have knowledge of business taxes?
A I have a good working knowledge of the relevant taxes. ☐
B I have some idea as to what taxes apply. ☐
C I do not know what taxes there are. ☐

Do you have bookkeeping knowledge?
A I understand double-entry bookkeeping. ☐
B I know a bit about single-entry bookkeeping. ☐
C I do not know how to do bookkeeping. ☐

Do you have knowledge of business budgets?
A I have been responsible for budgets and costings. ☐
B I have helped with budgets and/or costings. ☐
C I do not know how to do budgets and costings.* ☐
(Score 1 point if you have done domestic budgets satisfactorily.)*

Do you have knowledge of business laws?
A I know the laws that apply to my business. ☐
B I know about some of the laws. ☐
C I really do not know which laws apply. ☐

Do you have experience of managing staff?
A I have been a manager for many years. ☐
B I have had to supervise staff for several years. ☐
C I have little or no experience of managing staff.* ☐
*(*Score 1 point if you have led a sports team or club.)*

Do you have computer skills?
A I have good computer skills and knowledge of e-commerce. ☐
B I have some computer skills. ☐
C I have few or no computer skills.* ☐
*(*Score 1 point if you have access to a computer at home.)*

Results

0–10 points
You have a lot to learn even before you start your own business.

11–20 points
Although you have some skills and knowledge, you still have much to learn.

21–30 points
Your skills and knowledge may be reasonable, but find ways of filling the gaps.

31–40 points
Your business skills and knowledge appear to be satisfactory, but don't be complacent.

GETTING INTO THE RIGHT BUSINESS

Once you have decided that starting your own business suits your abilities and is what you really want to do, then you need to consider what sort of business you are going to run. In fact you may have thought initially of the business you wanted to start and then considered if it was the right step for you. This chapter looks at ways of finding a good business idea if you are starting from scratch, then covers some options for going into business using an existing framework: by direct selling, taking on a franchise, or buying a business that is already up and running.

The basis of your business is a business idea – one that is likely to be viable and, when put into practice, will give you a good quality of life in more than just financial terms. You might think that coming up with such an idea is purely a matter of inspiration, with the lucky entrepreneur waking up in the middle of the night with the plan fully formed that will make him or her into a millionaire. That happens on the odd occasion, but it is the exception rather than the rule. Often chance throws up a business opportunity, but the real skill is in recognizing it when it happens and then having the courage to do something about it.

Keep your focus on finding a product or service for which there is a market

Deciding what your business is going to do usually requires a good deal of hard thought and careful research. When you have come up with a business idea, subject it to broad and detailed scrutiny; develop the idea as far as you can to get a feel of its essential viability. The importance of finding a business for which there is a market need cannot be stressed too highly. Anyone can start up a business, but if there is not a sufficient need for its products or services then that business will fail – all too many businesses go under simply because there are too few customers. Your business idea will have a better chance of success if you can develop a

---

CASE STUDY: Starting to Form a Plan

HELEN AND JAMES had wanted to start a business together for some time. Helen had worked at management level with a major department store, and James had done a number of jobs using his accounting qualification. They both thought there was scope to open a quality gift shop in their town because it was a major tourist destination; with their respective training they felt they had the expertise to make it work. Although they considered the possibility of acquiring a franchise or buying an existing business, neither was available, so they had to start from scratch. This would be more risky but would allow them to plan and do things their own way, which they found appealing. Finding the right site would be one of their biggest challenges.

"unique selling proposition" (or USP) – a product or service that customers cannot obtain elsewhere. The whole business does not need to be unique, but you must offer something that is different, such as the style or speed of your service, or the manner in which you package your products. If your business idea passes this basic test, then you can undertake more detailed market research (see pp. 28–39) to help quantify and remove some of the risk of starting a business.

Think also at this stage about your business status: will you work alone, in a partnership, or as a limited company (see pp. 162–4)?

Starting from Nothing

If you are thinking of setting up in business but have not yet thought of what to do, there are a number of means that you can use to come up with a business idea.

COPYING AN EXISTING IDEA

This is probably the most common way a business idea is conceived. You might see a product or service that is not available locally, and decide that you could fill the gap by introducing it to your area. Almost every shop is an example of this, but there are many other possibilities such as leisure activities, local magazines, and so on. To gain inspiration, you could visit another area or city, or even travel abroad. Towns and cities abroad can be a rich source of business ideas, trends, and products. Take time to walk around the streets, look in the shops, watch the TV commercials, and read the papers and magazines. Of course, not everything that is a success elsewhere will be a success in your area. That is where market research is essential.

One form of copying that is not usually recommended is to mimic an established local business and set up in direct competition. This will work only if you are convinced that the

---

DEVELOPING YOUR BASIC BUSINESS IDEA

1 Describe your product or service in as much detail as you can.

2 Be clear about what you are offering that is different from others.

3 Think of your intended market; try to define its limits both geographically and in terms of the types of customers.

4 Look at options for selling your product or service – via a shop, distributors, by telephone, over the internet, and so on.

5 If your business is based on selling a product, will you manufacture it, or find someone else to do so?

6 Think what you may need to start in terms of premises, staff, equipment, finances, and expertise.

7 Be critical of your idea; try to spot and resolve potential flaws.

---

other business has serious weaknesses and that you can do it much better. You need to be sure that potential customers will back you by changing their allegiance, or that there is room for two such businesses.

SPIN-OFFS FROM WORK

Many new businesses are started by ex-employees who set up to do on their own as consultants or outsourcers what they were doing as employees. Frequently their ex-employer is one of their first customers. Other employees notice a business opportunity in the course of their work. For example, a salesperson might find a need among their customers for something that is not currently being sold. Or a designer working on one product may realize that a variant of that product has quite a different use and so set up a new business to exploit that. Alternatively, he or she might think of a significant improvement to an existing product which, if it were to go into production, would take a good share of the market. (Legal advice may be required to avoid infringing any patents.) Their position gives them inside information, they have the appropriate trade knowledge, and can choose their timing, so the chances of success are good. In some cases the spin-off may benefit their original employer by providing them with a service or product that they need.

BUILDING ON PERSONAL EXPERIENCE

This is often a good way to stumble on to business ideas, a personal experience having revealed a market gap. For example, a pregnant woman might find it hard to buy interesting maternity clothes, and so decide to set up a mail-order clothes business to meet the needs of that market.

ARTS AND CRAFTS

Trying to start a profitable business based on your artistic talents is difficult for a number of reasons, including finding enough outlets to distribute your products widely. You will need to allocate enough time for (and, if necessary, develop skills in) selling and distribution in addition to the time needed to produce your creative work. Often an artist or craftsperson may be selling works part-time; it is a big leap to transform this into a full-time livelihood. On the other hand, starting on a part-time basis allows you to develop contacts and assess the potential market.

INVENTIONS

There is a widespread belief that coming up with an original invention will lead to success in business. The fact is that few businesses start

---

INTELLECTUAL PROPERTY RIGHTS

If you have come up with an invention or new design on which to found your business, it is well worth trying to protect it with a patent or by other legal means. Note that you can only protect something physical; it is not possible to protect an idea.

■ **PATENT** A patent gives an inventor the right, for a limited period, to stop others from copying the idea without the inventor's permission. Patents generally relate to products, processes, mechanisms, materials, and so on that contain new functional or technical aspects. To be patentable, an invention must be new, involve an inventive step, be capable of industrial application, and not be on the exclusion list (discoveries, aesthetic creations, and computer programs are all on the list). Meeting these criteria can be difficult and the whole process of taking out a patent

can be costly and complex, particularly the necessary searches to ensure no one has patented a similar invention before. It is advisable to contact a registered patent agent at an early stage; look in the Yellow Pages to find your nearest patent agent. Note that patents are territorial, so you have to apply for one in each country where you wish to have your invention protected. Registering a patent discloses your invention publicly to others.

■ **REGISTERED DESIGN** The term "registered design" relates to the outward appearance of an article or a set of articles of manufacture.

AN EARLY HOOVER
This Hoover is an example of a patented invention whose name has become synonymous with vacuum cleaners. It is vital to patent such innovations to protect against illegal copying.

this way and, although some have been hugely successful, it is not an easy path to tread. If you have come up with and designed a new device, this is only the first hurdle. You then need either to find a keen manufacturer or to raise the funds to manufacture the device yourself, and start to carve out a niche in the marketplace among customers, many of whom are naturally conservative and wary of new things. To launch an innovative product requires substantial promotional or advertising budgets.

BUILDING ON HOBBIES AND SPORTS

Sometimes business opportunities arise from a hobby or sport. In this situation, success requires the entrepreneur to have a fair amount of experience in the sport or activity to know what is required. For example, a model aircraft competition winner might open a model shop. In particular, many good sportsmen and sportswomen use their talents to make money outside their sport but related to it. Golf professionals, for instance, may open golf shops. Their experience allows them to know what products to stock, their reputation can be used to publicize the enterprise, and their

---

To be registrable, the design must have significant eye appeal, be new, and not be excluded (for example, a work of sculpture would be on the exclusion list). Again, it is best to contact a patent agent for further information.

■ **TRADEMARK** A trademark can be applied to words, logos, or three-dimensional shapes that can distinguish the products (or services) of a particular business and can be represented graphically. Trademarks provide protection for the goodwill and reputation of a firm. Applications are usually handled by either a patent agent or trademark agent.

■ **COPYRIGHT** The concept of copyright relates to original literary, dramatic, musical, and artistic works (including paintings, photos, sculptures, works of architecture, technical drawings, maps, and logos), films and sound recordings, computer programs, and material on the internet. Often no registration is required to receive protection of copyright, but it is vital to have proof of the date of origination. Protection is automatic and immediate, but it may be advisable to use the copyright symbol © together with the date the work was first created.

■ **DESIGN RIGHT** Although registering a design gives you the strongest protection, there is automatic "design right" for certain designs, which does not require registration. Unlike copyright, the protection afforded by design right is effective only in the UK. Design right applies to original, non-commonplace designs of the shape or configuration of articles, so two-dimensional designs such as textiles will not qualify, although they would qualify for copyright protection.

advice will be appreciated by customers. There is a risk with this approach that a business is started more for the love of the sport or hobby than to meet a clear market need, and will never earn more than pin money. Bear in mind, too, that some people who have turned their hobby or sport into a business find that, though it works financially, it eventually spoils their love for the activity.

Consider direct selling only if you are self-motivated and gregarious

time. The manufacturers give their salespeople various titles, such as "distributors", "associates", "consultants", or "demonstrators"; these titles are sometimes prefixed by the word "independent". Many products are sold in this way, including clothes, cosmetics, household goods, jewellery, books, and dietary and nutritional products. Almost 90 per cent of the sales are made on a person-to-person basis, with the balance being by party plan. Ideally, to enter direct sales, you need to know a lot of people who can be your initial sales contacts.

Starting Up in Direct Selling

One way to start your own business within an existing structure is by direct selling. The process of direct selling is where a manufacturer misses out the retailer by selling direct to the consumer. These sales are usually made by self-employed people, who are generally home-based and often work part-

WARNING SIGNS IN A DIRECT-SALES FIRM

1 The company promises that you will "get rich quick".

2 Products are unsaleable, unattractive, overpriced, or of poor quality.

3 You would not choose to use their products yourself.

4 It is not clear exactly what you will be getting from the company until you have made an initial payment.

5 Earnings are primarily made by recruitment of new distributors rather than by selling actual products.

6 The company asks you for fixed, regular payments.

7 The company has not been trading for very long.

ADVANTAGES OF DIRECT SELLING

Being involved with a direct-selling company has many advantages over setting up a business on your own. Doing the market research, developing and testing new products, planning, pricing, and working out sales techniques are all done by the company. All you need do is to absorb their sales training and sometimes to purchase a starter pack of goods to sell. The sales procedure has been written by experts, so if you follow the training you should, in theory, be able to make sales.

PITFALLS TO AVOID

There are a number of reasons why people have difficulties in making a living from direct selling – that is, they don't make sufficient sales:

■ Not following the company's instructions.
■ Not allowing enough time (you need to commit yourself for as long as 12 months to give it a chance).
■ Becoming disenchanted with the cycle of selling and absorbing the company hype.
■ Working for a company that does not have a code of ethics – this implies an unprofessional attitude and, if goods are shoddy or fail to arrive as promised, end-users become disgruntled.
■ Working for a company that has unsaleable goods (a not uncommon problem).

CHOOSING A COMPANY

Joining a direct-selling company is usually quite easy. The relevant trade associations can give you the names of their member companies or you may already know a distributor. It is important that you like what the company has to sell and will use the products yourself, rather than just selling them to others.

NETWORK MARKETING

Some, though not all, direct-selling companies operate a multi-level system of sales where a salesperson can recruit other salespeople and will then receive bonuses depending on how well their recruits perform. This way of selling is called network marketing (networking) or multi-level marketing (MLM for short) and it

HOW IS DIRECT SELLING DONE?

Before getting involved in direct selling, it is important to know the main types of selling and how each one of them works.

■ **DOOR TO DOOR** This type of selling tends to operate by the salesperson leaving a catalogue and then returning a few days later hoping to take an order and pick up the catalogue. Success tends to rely on repeat business. Typically the salesperson gets about 20 per cent commission on each sale.

■ **SELLING TO CONTACTS** This is also known as "personal referral". You find the people who are interested in obtaining the product, visit them, and try to make a sale. The idea is that by making contact before you visit you know they are interested in the product, so it is not "cold calling", and you have a reasonable chance of making a sale. The key is to know a lot of people and be prepared to approach them all. You might contact neighbours, friends, relatives, people who are in clubs that you belong to, people in a religious group of which you are a member, parents of children with yours at school, and (where applicable) contact lists that you receive from your company. Be warned, though, that not everyone likes to be on the receiving end of this form of selling, so choose who you approach carefully.

DOOR-TO-DOOR SELLING
Some of the most successful door-to-door selling is done when a salesperson has built up a foundation of regular customers to visit.

■ **PARTY PLAN** This form of selling is still sometimes referred to as "Tupperware parties", after the company that first popularized it. A host – the salesperson or a friend of theirs – invites a group of friends and relatives to his or her home. The salesperson (or "demonstrator") brings samples of the items for sale, demonstrates them, and encourages the guests to place orders. Some people who sell in this way prefer to hold stock so the customers can take away their goods. Others take orders and then supply the goods later, collecting the money when the goods are handed over. Party-plan selling relies on good demonstration rather than a hard sell.

ASSESSING A FRANCHISE

WHAT TO LOOK FOR

A proven business format that is viable, with advertising support and an operations manual.

The use of a business name and/or trademark.

Training in both trade and business skills.

A contract that clearly defines the rights and obligations of both parties.

Long-term market research to ensure that the business keeps up with marketplace changes.

An exclusive territory large enough to generate sufficient income.

Full support before, during, and after start-up, including ongoing advice and troubleshooting.

WHAT TO AVOID

Only one outlet in the country (the franchise is not fully proven).

Sales pitch based on the success of the franchise in another country.

The franchisor does a hard sell on you.

Huge projected profits from a small set-up fee.

Large initial fee.

Claims there is little selling to do (this is unlikely).

Territories mapped out, without researching the different areas of the country and their very differing markets.

A dismissive attitude towards competitors.

accounts for about a quarter of total direct sales. It works like this: you sell the products to friends and contacts. One or two of them might think they can sell it to their friends and so agree to become distributors. By recruiting them, you earn bonuses that are dependent on their sales. If those new distributors recruit more people you get a share of their sales bonuses, too. This continues as the network expands. The people who recruit you are called your "uplines" and the people you recruit are your "downlines".

For achieving high sales levels, most direct-selling companies have prizes such as holidays, appliances, even cars. This is usually related to recruitment success as well as individual sales. Some people (a small minority) do achieve high incomes from this type of selling and the companies they work with are huge multi-billion-turnover concerns. Network marketing, along with other aspects of direct selling, is regulated by law (see p. 172).

Taking on a Franchise

In franchising, you copy someone else's business, with their full approval and support, under a licence agreement called a franchise. In this the franchise-giver (the franchisor) allows you to use their trade name, provides training and back-up, and gives their expertise with all its benefits. In exchange, you as the franchisee have to pay the franchisor an initial fee, then ongoing royalties. The major advantage of this method is that you get into business more quickly and possibly with less risk.

The franchise you take on should be a well-proven business idea; unfortunately, the success of franchising has attracted many unscrupulous businesspeople who are offering franchises of dubious value. There is therefore a need for caution and independent professional advice. Franchising was developed in the US in the 1950s, and many of the well-known franchise names are still American.

How Does Franchising Work?

Setting up any business takes money, but with a franchise operation it costs you more, because you are also paying for the business experience and proven product or service of the franchisor. In return they may set up the whole business for you, including taking care of all the legal work, training you and any partners and staff, and helping you to select stock and/or tools. In some cases this hand-holding is very complete, but you need to decide if the extra cost of a franchise is worthwhile.

The franchisor provides an operations manual, which lays down the whole format of how to run the business. There is also a contract, which forms the basis of the close association between yourself and the franchisor. Check this document very carefully, no matter how well-known the franchisor. Read all of it and ensure you understand it. Ask questions about any part you do not understand. Before you sign it, consult a solicitor – some contracts have hostile clauses that, should you have a problem running the business, are likely to work in favour of the franchisor rather than you.

How to Assess a Franchise

Many franchisors are members of a national association, which you can contact for information, and there are a number of franchising magazines available. To meet franchisors, there are various franchise exhibitions held annually. When you have found several franchises that interest you, get their free information packs (also called prospectuses). Each should describe the franchise in detail. If your bank has a franchise unit, get their advice. The next step is to visit the franchisor's head office.

If satisfied so far, ask to see a specimen contract and take it away to read carefully and show it to your solicitor. After the meeting, visit at least two of their franchisees (of your own choice) and get their viewpoint. Now do your own market research (see pp. 28–39). You need to find out just how strong the market demand is for such products or services, what customers think of the franchise, and the strength of the competition in your area.

A common complaint is that franchisors understate the necessary capital to start the business. They sometimes entirely omit your living costs prior to the business making a profit, they may quote a low figure to purchase a second-hand van or other piece of essential equipment, and omit your own legal and accountancy fees. VAT is also often omitted: you will have to pay this and can claim it back only if you are going to be VAT-registered yourself.

Taking on a franchise does not guarantee success. Some franchises fail altogether, while others do not meet projected turnover figures.

Questions to Ask a Franchisor

When you visit a franchisor, ask probing questions – even if some are answered in their prospectus – and note down the answers.

- When was the business established?
- Are they members of the national franchise association? And, if not, why?
- How many outlets are there in the country?
- How many outlets have ceased trading, and why?
- What are the credentials of the people behind the franchise?
- How good is the company's financial performance?
- What is the initial capital required?
- What are the addresses of franchisees you can visit?
- How is the royalty calculated?
- What do you get for your money?
- What ongoing support do they give?
- Are there other charges, e.g. advertising?
- What are the long-term prospects for the franchise?
- What is the length of the agreement and how can it be terminated?
- Who is the competition?

A FRANCHISE

Pizza Hut is an example of an international franchise. Many international franchises originate in North America. Other franchises are on a smaller scale and are confined to a particular country.

A franchisor's membership of a national franchise association does not lessen the need for careful checking on your part. Even if you join a good, well-managed, ethical franchise, your own business could still have problems due to local competition and trading circumstances. Franchising works for many thousands of people, but it is essential to choose your franchise very carefully indeed. Even if it is successful, the business will require plenty of hard work and some considerable time to become established.

Buying an Existing Business

This is a popular way to get into business and can be highly successful, as it shortcuts much of the difficult start-up process. Businesses are sold by word of mouth, and advertised in local newspapers and specialist publications. Shop sales are also handled by business transfer agents.

To buy a viable existing business you need to do your homework thoroughly and to maintain an open, yet cynical mind. Why cynical? Because one must examine why a good small business is being sold. If the business is doing even reasonably well, it is more likely to be taken over by a close friend or a member of the proprietor's family, or the proprietor could employ a manager. That is not to say that good or potentially good businesses do not come on to the market, but you need be fully aware of what you are taking on and why it is being sold.

First, ensure you are well informed about the trade and the type of business you are contemplating taking over. Contact your local business development unit for their advice and ask if they can put you in touch with a similar business far enough away not to be in direct competition. Consult books and trade publications. If you are still interested, then the next step is to value the business for sale.

DOING YOUR RESEARCH

Obtain good advice from an accountant, who should go through the last few years' accounts of the business and explain to you all the salient features. Be sure you also understand any tax and VAT implications of the purchase.

By buying an existing business you have access to their real trading figures, so you can make better cash flow and profit predictions than if you were starting from scratch. But trading conditions vary constantly and you must still do thorough market research to ensure that market conditions are not likely to vary adversely for the foreseeable future. If there are any existing staff, look carefully at their terms, conditions, and rates of pay as you will have to observe these. If you plan to reduce the number of staff, you could be liable for redundancy payments.

Enquire fully into the situation regarding the premises. Are the premises owned by the business or rented? If rented, then check the lease carefully (see pp. 69–70). It is essential for a structural survey to be done and to find out if you would be responsible for the repairs and insurance of the building. The surveyor can also comment on the lease prior to you consulting your solicitor.

If the business you are buying is a limited company, you will need to obtain excellent legal advice, because when you take on a company (usually by the purchase of a majority of its shares) you take on not only the assets, but also all of its liabilities, which might be substantial. Ideally, and wherever possible, you should aim to acquire the assets rather than the company itself.

Valuing a Business

Every business has its strengths and weaknesses. In general terms, however, the value of a business (what you have to pay) is the sum of the following four factors:

■ **Stock** This is best valued independently (not by the seller). All businesses suffer from dead stock – stock that is unlikely to be sold as it is either out of date, damaged, or was never saleable in the first place. The valuation should therefore be the depreciated cost price (not retail price) of the saleable goods.
■ **Fixtures and Fittings** Again these should be valued independently, taking into account their value after depreciation.
■ **Machinery and Equipment** This is valued like fixtures and fittings.
■ **Goodwill** Whereas the above categories can be valued precisely (though may still be subject to disputes), goodwill is the grey area of valuation and is highly negotiable. Goodwill equals the value of the business less the tangible business assets. It is a measure of the momentum of profitability that the business has built up. It should therefore be based on the proven profit of the business, looking at the last few years (since the business may be growing rapidly or declining). If a typical net profit (before-tax) figure can be agreed on, then the goodwill for a small business can usually be valued at between one and five times the profit figure. The actual multiplier chosen is dependent upon all the other factors involved in the sale, such as the perceived growth potential of the business, any patents or designs owned by the business, the quality and training of staff, and the size of the existing customer base. The larger the business, the greater the multiplier used when calculating the goodwill. If it relates closely to the personality and reputation of the former owner, that part will be lost when he or she leaves and so the business will be worth less. Note that in simple terms if the goodwill is, for instance, three times the net profit of the business, it will take you three years just to recoup that money, and that assumes the business continues to generate the same profits.

Fact File

Depreciation is the amount by which equipment is diminished each year. If depreciation is 25 per cent, the depreciated "book value" of a £100 asset will be £75 after one year, £56.25 after two years, and so on. The depreciated value of an item is often less than it might be worth to a buyer, so a balance needs to be struck when valuing a business.

will be sustained for long periods. Rely on an overview of your own market research to guide you.

Even if your proposed business does not need a national-sized market to sustain it, national trends can have a significant effect at a local level. You need to know if the market you are entering is expanding, contracting, stable, or very dependent upon another market, which itself is changing rapidly. Markets tend to start slowly, expand rapidly, then plateau, or sometimes decline. Businesses that offer a new product or service early on when the market is expanding often do much better than those that come along later in the life of the market, but the early entrepreneurs are exposed to greater risk. The way to find out which stage your market is at is through desk research.

Write down the questions you need to ask before a meeting

There may also be legislation in the pipeline that could have a major effect on your plans. If in doubt, contact the relevant trade association for information.

LOCAL RESEARCH

Once you have built up some knowledge of the national situation and relevant trends, you need to find out much more about the trade on a local level. To this end there is no better source of information than the trade itself. Speak to the sales representatives of your likely suppliers – they can provide good information if asked the correct questions. Try to find out from them about consistent long-term sellers as well as what is popular right now. Contact your local business development unit, and ask if they can put you in touch with someone who is working

PITFALLS TO AVOID WHEN DOING MARKET RESEARCH

PITFALL	HOW TO AVOID IT
OVERCONFIDENCE Being convinced that your product or service will work	Take any warning signs or negative feedback seriously. If potential customers display no interest as you do your research, ask them why, and try to accommodate their suggestions. Above all, keep an open mind.
IMPRECISION Failing to define your target market	Usually 20 per cent of the customers provide 80 per cent of the turnover. Aim to identify and focus on the few key customers.
PRICE CUTTING Assuming that cutting prices will allow you to compete successfully	The buying decision is a complex one – look at all the alternatives. Factors such as quality, guarantees, and speed of service influence the sale as much as price.
SHORT-TERM THINKING Underestimating how long it will take to enter a market and obtain a reasonable market share	Obtaining a market share takes years not months. It is hard to estimate the reactions of competitors, but the only safe strategy is to assume that they will react aggressively, and to plan accordingly.
COMPLACENCY Being too reliant on contacts who promise to supply work when you start	Ask yourself how they manage without you now. Ask your contacts for more details of their needs, and for estimates of orders to test their genuineness.

in the same business but located in a different part of the country (so that you would not be in direct competition).

YOUR TARGET MARKET

Next you need to consider the "target market" – the section of the population that could potentially use your product or service. Aim to define in detail who your customers are, their needs, and what benefit they will derive from using your product or service. They are obviously surviving without you at present so why will they want to use your business in future? Also, are there enough potential customers within reach of your business?

At this point, you need to be clear about whether your customers will be other businesses (trade), or whether you will sell direct to the general public, or both. Business customers generally have larger budgets and different requirements, such as the precise date by which a service must be completed, or specific details relating to the design of the packaging. They also expect credit, whereas a private customer is usually prepared to pay immediately, which can have a significant effect on your cash flow.

Talk direct to potential buyers – there is no substitute

If your target market is business customers, first prepare a list of some or all of the businesses that may be interested in your product or service. Get their names from Yellow Pages, or a similar local business directory, then find out the name of the best person in the firm to approach. Contact them and find out their views on what you have to offer.

In contrast, if your target market is private customers, trying to find out who will buy what from you is much more difficult. In this case, start by asking people already in the same business (where they are not direct competitors) for their views and advice. The next step is to speak directly to likely customers and the most thorough way of doing that with the public is with a questionnaire.

Using Questionnaires

A questionnaire is the best way to find out about the needs, views, and habits of local customers in a structured manner. There are five golden rules to follow to compile effective questionnaires:

1 **KEEP IT SHORT AND SIMPLE** Ask yourself what it is you are really trying to find out. Concentrate on the most important questions and avoid any fringe issues. There should be no more than five to ten questions. A multiple-choice or Yes/No format is best as it is both easier to answer and quicker to analyze.

2 **AVOID LOADED QUESTIONS** This is best illustrated with an example. If you were considering buying a mobile shop, then you might ask householders in the appropriate district their views, to assess if the business would be viable. A question such as "Do you buy anything from a mobile shop at present?" would be reasonable. Asking "Would you use a mobile shop if it were cheaper than the local shop?" is a loaded question, and invites a positive reply. It is very easy to fall into the trap of asking such questions. Also, try to avoid emotive or exaggerated phrases in the question. Be aware that, out of politeness, people often give the reply that they think you want to hear.

3 **MINIMIZE OPEN QUESTIONS** The purpose of the questionnaire is to pose specific questions that you have thought out carefully so that the answers allow you to draw firm conclusions. The danger of an open question (such as "Do you think mobile shops are a good idea?") is that it could lead to a long debate. There is, of course, value in open questions: the responses can reveal useful and relevant factors of which you are unaware. The best

PREPARING A BUSINESS PLAN

One of the first steps in starting any new business should be the preparation of a business plan – a detailed planning document that sets out in both words and figures a proposed business venture. This can either be a new business start-up or a major expansion or diversification of an existing business. A business plan is as essential to the business that requires only £1,000 to set up as to one that needs £1 million. The principal role of a business plan is to persuade potential backers that your business is a sound proposition; it also helps you to plan and monitor the progress of your business.

A business plan should be drafted by the people behind the venture, with appropriate advice from an accountant. The purposes of a business plan are to:
■ transfer your thoughts to paper
■ raise finance
■ monitor the project.

Spend time on your business plan – it is for your benefit as much as a financial backer's

you do the necessary research. The business plan is the key to open financiers' coffers and so must contain all the information that is needed to answer their likely questions. It should also be neatly presented and clearly laid out. The document should be persuasive in tone, conveying your enthusiasm for the project, and it

KEY PURPOSES

When you start to plan how to set up a new business, there are many aspects to consider. By putting down the business idea in a structured plan, the situation will become clearer and you can start to assess the project more objectively. Furthermore, to complete the plan you will have to answer a lot of questions and this will make

should emphasize the four key aspects that financial backers look for:
■ evidence of market research
■ proper planning
■ financial control
■ competence and commitment of the people behind the project.

CASE STUDY: Producing a Planning Tool

AFTER A CAREER in education, then industry, Margaret decided to set up her own training company. She had completed sufficient market research to conclude that there was a shortage of trainers in her area, and that there was enough work if she could market her company well. Although she was funding the venture entirely by herself, she decided to produce a business plan. This would help her to gather her thoughts and focus on exactly who she should be approaching to find training work, what her charges should be, and how much income she needed to cover her operating costs. She found that producing a break-even cash-flow forecast for her business plan was a great comfort, as she knew that if she met those monthly targets she would survive.

Even if you do not need to borrow money in order to start up your business, the business plan could save you from losing your own funds, since the detailed financial forecasting required to complete the plan should help to show up any potential problems in advance.

The plan lays down the path along which the business should be moving, for at least the first year – sometimes longer. When a business is starting up there are so many things to do that it is easy to delude yourself that the business is doing well just because you are busy. With the business plan at your side, you can take stock of the situation, at least monthly, and check to see if you are still progressing along the planned path (particularly in terms of the cash-flow

forecast). If not, remedial action can be taken, the sooner the better. Cash-flow management is discussed in more detail on pp. 140–42.

Choosing a Format for Your Business Plan

A number of different formats are suitable for a business plan, athough the information contained within each will be broadly similar. There is also software available for generating business plans in which you answer set questions and the program creates the plan for you. These programs have obvious advantages (such as ease) and disadvantages (such as inflexibility),

PULLING TOGETHER RESEARCH
Writing your business plan involves gathering all the research you have done so far, looking critically at it, and making use of the information that is relevant. You will also need to do some additional research to provide a full picture.

INTRODUCTION

This is a clear statement outlining the nature of the proposed business. For a manufacturer, the plan needs to mention the product's current stage of development and, if it is already in production, when it was first launched and how many have been sold. For a service venture, the plan needs to state if the business is a retailer, wholesaler, or whatever is relevant. If several phases of development are envisaged, this should also be mentioned.

BUSINESS HISTORY

Not included in this example, the business history section is needed only where an existing business is being bought or if the business plan is for a firm that is already trading and is planning a major expansion or diversification. This section would mention the date the business started (usually the date of incorporation for a limited company) and note any major recent events in the history of the business. In addition, the business history text

---

INTRODUCTION
Here the purpose and scope of the business is stated briefly, along with a mention that the plan is aimed at raising finance for the business.

Target market is clearly stated as the "over 50s age group"

Makes clear the need for the business among customers

Size of market is defined by stating population of town, and potential catchment area

Potential competition is listed with strengths and weaknesses

---

BUSINESS PLAN: SIMPLY PERFECT

INTRODUCTION

The objective is to set up a ladies' fashion shop in the town centre. The shop will stock ladies' fashions aimed mainly at the over 50s age group. Garments will include dresses, skirts, blouses, coats, hosiery, hats, and accessories, and will be in styles and sizes appropriate to that target market. The purpose of this plan is to raise the finance for the venture.

MARKET RESEARCH

During her years in retail in the area, Joan Smith has observed that many of her older clientele complained that they were obliged to travel to the city, some 28 miles away, to find good clothes shops. This prompted her to investigate the market further. The population of the town is 66,500 but, with several smaller towns nearby, the potential market is larger. The existing shops in the area that might present competition to her venture are as follows:

ICEBERGS — A large department store catering to a wide age group with only a limited range for the over 50s in its ladieswear department, though there is good availability of sizes and high stock levels.

CITY FASHIONS — A new upmarket shop but with relatively high prices, and fashions more appropriate to younger customers. Little stock is held in larger sizes.

3

would comment on the business's current financial position and refer to the latest accounts (a copy of which would be enclosed at the back of the business plan). For larger projects the last three years' accounts may be required.

MARKET RESEARCH

Vitally important, this section, in most cases, should take at least a page of text and generally much more, especially with larger projects. This part of the plan summarizes the findings of the market research, including target customers, the size of the market and any assumptions you have made about it, how sensitive the market is to price, and an outline of the competition and their strengths and weaknesses. Pricing policy specifics can be covered in the financial section later.

For larger projects an independent market research report will give credibility to the plan; this would be attached to the business plan and referred to as necessary in the text.

BUSINESS PLAN: SIMPLY PERFECT

TOWN TRENDS   A small shop stocking fashions mainly aimed at younger customers, and priced at the middle to lower end of the range.

MISS JONES   A small boutique with only skirts and dresses for this age group. Joan Smith used to work in this shop.

There is at present little direct competition from shops in the town or nearby. The main competitors are the shops in the city. Joan Smith has questioned a sample of 50 women whom she knows and who would all be potential customers of her new store. Of this sample, 44 said they would be interested in a local fashion shop in preference to others 28 miles away in the city. The only reservations were expressed by six women whose work took them to the city anyway and who felt they would probably continue to visit the shops there.

In terms of price sensitivity, Joan Smith's retail experience indicates that her target market is relatively affluent and tends to be more concerned about the style, quality, and fit of clothing, rather than its price.

4

MARKET RESEARCH

This section covers all the key points connected with the market, showing that thorough research has been done to prove there is a potential customer base for the shop.

Text covers attitudes of members of target market to all relevant competition in catchment area

Indicates that other factors are more important than price for potential market

CASH-FLOW FORECAST

Usually created using a computer spreadsheet, the cash-flow forecast is a key element of the business plan. A cash flow forecast is just what it says – a prediction of the cash flowing in and out of the business, usually on a monthly basis. This forecast is normally done for 12 months, though a project with long lead times may need a 24- or 36-month forecast. In that case, years two and three tend to have the forecast done on a quarterly basis, as greater accuracy is unlikely.

The preparation of the cash-flow forecast requires estimates and assumptions, which should be explained in the business plan, together with hard facts derived from your research. The procedure for creating a cash-flow forecast is given on pages 56–7.

The golden rule with a cash-flow forecast is to be pessimistic and not underestimate your overheads

Rarely, if ever, is a cash-flow forecast right first time. That does not diminish its importance, for the process of compiling the first cash flow forecast forces you to face up to some harsh realities and make a number of important decisions. What makes a cash-flow forecast such an important tool for planning and controlling your finances is that you can update it regularly (at least monthly), and you can also experiment by inserting different figures to envisage different scenarios.

FACT FILE

If it is very difficult to forecast your sales, do a break-even cash flow. Complete the whole cash flow, leaving the "sales" line until the very end. Then insert what sales you have to make to break even – that is, ensuring the bottom line of the cash flow is positive or within the overdraft limit. You then know what level of sales you must achieve to survive.

HINTS TO COMPLETE A CASH FLOW

The following hints are intended to help you to complete your cash-flow forecast:

■ LINE 1 (SALES) Here you estimate your likely sales (turnover) for the year ahead. If you are offering credit, you should show the payments in the month when you expect to receive the cash.

■ LINE 20 (REPAIRS AND MAINTENANCE) Note that vehicle repairs are covered on line 17.

■ LINE 24 (STOCK/RAW MATERIALS) In many cases there will be an initial stocking-up phase, and subsequently this line should bear a relationship to the sales line since you cannot make sales without stock. If you are given credit by your suppliers, this can have a marked bearing on your cash flow.

■ LINE 30 (VAT) A small business may not need to register for VAT unless its turnover exceeds, or is likely to exceed, the current threshold figure. In the example, the fictitious shop has not registered for VAT so line 30 remains zero. For a VAT-registered business, line 30 is used for VAT payments made to Customs and Excise.

■ LINE 33 (NET CASH FLOW) This is line 5 less line 32. If the figure is positive it means that more cash was received than was spent during the month (good). If negative, more cash was spent than received (not good).

■ LINE 34 (OPENING BALANCE) This always starts at 0 for a new business, and each subsequent month equals the closing balance of the previous month.

■ LINE 35 (CLOSING BALANCE) This is the forecast cash in the bank at the end of each month. If this line is negative, it means your bank account will be overdrawn. Either you need an overdraft, or you will need to cut down on expenses or boost sales income to get yourself "out of the red". The totals in this line represent neither a profit nor a loss. If you can keep the amount in this line positive (or at least within your overdraft limit), you will not run out of cash.

CASH-FLOW FORECAST: SIMPLY PERFECT

CASH IN	MAY	JUN	JUL	AUG	SEP	OCT	NOV	DEC	JAN	FEB	MAR	APR	TOTALS
1 SALES	1,500	2,000	4,000	6,000	4,000	3,000	5,500	10,000	1,500	2,500	4,000	4,500	48,500
2 BANK OR OTHER LOANS	0	4,000	0	0	0	0	0	0	0	0	0	0	4,000
3 OWNER'S CAPITAL	10,000	0	0	0	0	0	0	0	0	0	0	0	10,000
4 OTHER MONEY IN	0	0	0	0	0	0	0	0	0	0	0	0	0
5 TOTAL CASH IN	11,500	6,000	4,000	6,000	4,000	3,000	5,500	10,000	1,500	2,500	4,000	4,500	62,500
CASH OUT													
6 ADVERTISING AND PROMOTION	300	0	0	0	0	0	500	0	0	0	0	0	800
7 BANK CHARGES/INTEREST	0	50	50	100	50	50	50	72	50	50	50	50	622
8 BUSINESS INSURANCES	500	0	0	0	0	0	0	0	0	0	0	0	500
9 BUSINESS RENT	1,000	0	0	1,000	0	0	1,000	0	0	1,000	0	0	4,000
10 BUSINESS RATES	0	400	400	400	400	400	400	400	400	400	400	0	4,000
11 CLEANING	0	0	0	0	0	0	0	0	0	0	0	0	0
12 DRAWINGS/SALARIES/NIC	0	500	500	750	750	750	1,000	1,000	750	1,000	1,000	1,000	9,000
13 ELECTRIC/GAS/HEAT/WATER	0	150	0	0	150	0	0	150	0	0	150	0	600
14 FINANCE CHARGES	0	160	160	160	160	160	160	160	160	160	160	160	1760
15 LEGAL AND PROFESSIONAL	450	0	0	0	0	0	0	0	0	0	0	400	850
16 MOTOR - FUEL	0	0	0	0	0	0	0	0	0	0	0	0	0
17 MOTOR - OTHER EXPENSES	0	0	0	0	0	0	0	0	0	0	0	0	0
18 OTHER EXPENSES	0	0	0	0	0	0	0	0	0	0	0	0	0
19 POSTAGE/PARCELS	0	0	0	0	0	0	0	0	0	0	0	0	0
20 REPAIRS AND MAINTENANCE	0	50	0	0	50	0	0	50	0	0	50	0	200
21 STAFF WAGES	0	0	0	0	0	0	0	0	0	0	0	0	0
22 STAFF PAYE/NIC	0	0	0	0	0	0	0	0	0	0	0	0	0
23 STATIONERY/PRINTING	50	10	10	10	10	10	10	10	10	10	10	10	160
24 STOCK/RAW MATERIALS	8,000	4,000	2,000	2,000	2,000	1,000	6,000	500	0	3,000	3,000	2,000	33,500
25 SUBSCRIPTIONS	0	0	0	0	0	0	0	0	0	0	0	0	0
26 SUNDRIES	80	50	30	20	20	20	40	30	20	20	20	20	370
27 TAX PAYMENTS	0	0	0	0	0	0	0	0	0	0	0	0	0
28 TELEPHONE/FAX	100	50	0	0	75	0	0	75	0	0	75	0	375
29 TRAVEL AND SUBSISTENCE	0	0	0	0	150	0	0	0	0	0	0	150	300
30 VAT	0	0	0	0	0	0	0	0	0	0	0	0	0
31 CAPITAL EXPENDITURE	3,350	0	0	0	0	0	0	0	0	0	0	0	3,350
32 TOTAL CASH OUT	13,830	5,420	3,150	4,440	3,815	2,390	9,160	2,447	1,390	5,640	4,915	3,790	60,387
33 NET CASH FLOW	-2,330	580	850	1,560	185	610	-3660	7,553	110	-3,140	-915	710	
34 OPENING BALANCE	0	-2,330	-1,750	-900	660	845	1,455	-2,205	5,348	5,458	2,318	1,403	
35 CLOSING BALANCE	-2,330	-1,750	-900	660	845	1,455	-2,205	5,348	5,458	2,318	1,403	2,113	

required. It is advisable to approach the relevant agency before you commence trading or set up your business, and your business plan should demonstrate a clear need for the assistance.

What government help there is comes from many sources (the EC, central and local government) and is channelled through many different bodies. It can also vary considerably from one area to another. For a significant majority of business start-ups there is little help available in terms of hard cash. Instead it may provide help with rent-free periods in industrial units, assistance with research and technology projects, and the training of staff, especially where these relate to the employment of long-term unemployed people, people with disabilities, or young people.

STOCK EXCHANGE

Equity financiers tend to invest in larger small businesses. Some equity financiers are large companies set up to invest in projects that they deem to be good risks – those likely to bring them a high return on their investment.

In addition to financial assistance available from government, there are a number of other organizations which may be able to assist new business start-ups. Their help can range from business advice and mentoring to financial assistance. Your local business development organization or local authority will be able to point you in the right direction to obtain government assistance, or alternatively provide the names of other organizations to which you can apply for financial help.

Funding from Equity Financiers

This type of funding is available only if you plan to set up a limited company. It involves obtaining investment money by selling shares in your company privately. There are two very good reasons for having an outside investor in your business – first, they can contribute business knowledge and contacts and, second,

by having the money invested as equity (shares) rather than loans you are not in danger of becoming overgeared (see box, above).

Many people want to retain total control and ownership of their new business because they are convinced that they will make their fortune from it and they do not feel inclined to share the spoils. However, it takes a good deal of investment and business acumen to make your fortune, and those elusive millions are much more easily obtained if you are prepared to have a slice of a large cake rather than the whole of a small one.

An investor should contribute knowledge as well as capital to your business, so choose these partners carefully and ask what they can offer by way of expertise, and trade and customer contacts, in addition to money.

Equity finance can come from one or a combination of two main sources: private investors or venture capitalists.

PRIVATE INVESTORS

An individual invests directly in the business by purchasing shares, which are often a nominal £1 each. If the total capital being invested is £20,000, there will be £20,000 of "issued share capital". You may have decided to invest £12,000 of your own (you will therefore own 60 per cent of the company), and to ask other shareholder(s) to invest the remaining £8,000. If you do not want to give up as much of the equity as this or you want more funds, then

Choose an investor you can get on with even if the going gets tough

you could top up with loans or set up more complicated financial structures. For example, different classes of shares can be issued, or a limited company can be split into several limited companies. Seek advice if you wish to find out more about these highly technical arrangements. Note that an investor is better protected if some of their money is in the form of a loan, because if the business fails they are more likely to get some of the loan money back, whereas the share capital is likely to be lost.

Private investors are sometimes known as "business angels". Generally you need to approach them and persuade them that your firm is a good one in which to invest. The drawbacks of accepting private investment are few, provided that you can work well with the individual in question, and accept that you are giving up (selling) part of your business.

VENTURE CAPITALISTS

Venture capitalists are individuals or companies (set up to invest in business) who may be interested in projects that are on the larger side of "small", with start-up capital in the £50,000-plus category, ideally more. You can find them through accountants, banks, or a local business development organization. Usually you have to pay fees for acquiring venture capital money. These may include "negotiation fees" (also called "commitment fees") for arranging the finance, which can vary from two to seven per cent. Together with legal fees, these administration costs can reach ten per cent of the sum raised. In addition, some organizations also charge annual "management fees". This makes it expensive money. However, an attractive aspect of equity finance is that companies, if empowered by their Articles of Association, can buy back their own shares out of capital, provided certain safeguards are met. This mechanism may attract investors, since they can make a capital gain and recover their hangers facing in opposite directions, thus preventing a thief from grabbing a whole rail in one go. High-value stock needs electronic tagging, an alarmed wire, or – even better still – a wire and small padlock.

One question to resolve is where to put spare stock. It may be that you resupply daily, or have a storeroom at the back of the shop, or perhaps use high-level shelving above the normal retail displays.

A key part of the interior layout is the salespoint, where the cash till is located. This needs to integrate with the rest of the layout. There are many schools of thought about the best location: having the till by the door allows staff to monitor customers; on the other hand, by the rear of the shop is more secure, and ensures that customers walk through the shop. The exact positioning needs careful thought and will depend on the shop space available, the planned layout, and the sort of business you are in. The choice of cash till needs to reflect your method of keeping your accounts, the sales information you want, and the requirements of the tax authorities.

EXTERIOR ASPECTS

The overall image that the shop projects sends an important signal to a potential customer and, as a result of that image, they may or may not choose to enter. Seeking professional advice is not simply about getting the shop "to look good", but making it actually work and be a viable business. Get the design wrong and the business will suffer badly or fail. Have a closer look at shops similar to the one you propose so that you can get an idea of what may be involved. In particular, look at branches of successful retail chains to see what their professional designers and shopfitters have done, and weigh up the task that confronts you.

Together with the shopfront and signage, window displays are critical in attracting customers. Professionally arranged window displays require props, which can be made or purchased from specialist suppliers. Sometimes sales representatives will provide sales material to promote their goods that you can use in your window displays. A good rule of thumb is to change the window display every week. This is not only a simple discipline to keep the shop's appearance interesting, but is based on the assumption that many people shop on a weekly basis. Note that any external signage may be subject to restrictions by landlords, mall operators, or local bylaws.

Equipping a Workshop or Small Industrial Unit

When you are buying equipment for an industrial unit, the key factors you must first consider are:

- storage of raw materials
- workflow
- storage of completed goods
- regulations
- security.

Storage can be a bigger problem than many anticipate, and the need here is to have ease of delivery coupled with ease of access for production. Most goods travel around the country loaded on pallets, though small quantities are usually packed in cartons. Your goods inwards area may require some form of pallet handling, though the alternative is to break a pallet down. There are plenty of solutions to handling goods, the snag being that the equipment, such as pallet trucks, fork-lifts, racking, and possibly conveyor systems,

WORKSHOP
The key to equipping a workspace is to ensure that the layout is geared towards ease of production. Here, a simple workbench has been situated by a window that provides good natural light.

can be quite expensive. However, if you need them, they should more than repay their cost in terms of efficiency. Another potential problem is protecting the goods from the weather and from damage due to poor handling, either while in storage or in transit.

In terms of workflow, the choice of equipment and its precise placement in the unit should be to facilitate efficient production and to establish a safe working environment. Compliance with the many safety regulations is essential and, unless you have experience in this field, it is vital to get professional advice. Experiment on paper with different layouts drawn to scale before finalizing your purchases. Industrial units are often the targets of thieves or vandals; this needs careful consideration and professional advice from security experts.

STARTING out

*L*aunching your venture means making potential customers aware of what your business has to offer, and beginning to make sales. Be prepared for a steep learning curve as you start to put your plans into action. A flexible attitude and a willingness to keep rethinking and improving on your business are essential. As your business grows, you may need to consider different ways of expanding at home or abroad.

MARKETING

You have a business only if you can make sales, and the whole process of getting those sales involves proper marketing. Good marketing is vital to every business. It covers the whole process of selling goods or services, including correct pricing, appropriate advertising, useful promotion, and, finally, effective selling. These four aspects need to be in harmony to work successfully, which is why a marketing strategy is essential for the best results. The first two aspects are covered in this chapter, while sales and promotion are covered on pages 98–113.

Doing the market research for your business should have enabled you to assess whether there is a market for your proposed business and if it is big enough to support you. Even if this is so, your business will not succeed unless you market it properly. Market research is a key element of marketing and should be an ongoing process once your business is up and running.

There are innumerable different ways to market your product or service. For instance, if you were publishing a trade magazine you could distribute it free and rely on the advertising revenue to make a profit, allowing you to guarantee a wide circulation to your advertisers. An alternative marketing strategy would be to charge readers a subscription; your circulation will be less, which might put off some advertisers, but you would have a more reliable income from the subscriptions. Even a fairly straightforward business can market itself in different ways. A high-street instant print shop, for example, could simply rely on passing trade, or the proprietor could go out and visit businesses to bring in more printing work. When you start your business you need to come up with a marketing strategy that relates to your market research and business plan. Once you start trading you can adjust and improve the strategy as necessary.

Spend time developing a marketing strategy

Pricing a Product or Service

The first basic aspect to consider is pricing. This is difficult to get right. A key element of working out pricing is understanding your costs. Once you know your costs, you can use this as an element in the pricing calculation. Two types of costs are relevant here:

■ **FIXED COSTS** Also known as overheads, these refer to business expenditure, which is basically constant or fixed irrespective of the level of trading. Rent, rates, most salaries, and insurance, are examples of fixed costs.

■ **VARIABLE COSTS** Also known as direct costs, these comprise expenditure which varies directly in relation to the level of business; for instance, the costs of raw materials.

The price you choose needs to meet your fixed and variable costs, and then make a surplus (your profit) on top. This is the minimum you need to make from your sales to stay in business. With fixed costs it therefore makes a good deal of difference whether you sell one item or a hundred items per year, or provide a service for one day or a hundred days, since the entire fixed costs have to be recovered on those sales. Dividing the fixed costs by one, a hundred, or whatever, obviously has a huge impact on the end price. Be very cautious in predicting your likely sales in terms of units sold or chargeable time.

Fixed costs must always be kept to a minimum as they can float upwards and soon overwhelm the profitability of a business (see pp. 142–4). Businesses are usually better at controlling their "variable costs". For example, when a supplier raises their prices, most businesses take notice and, where the rise is unjustified, they will challenge it or find a new supplier.

SENDING THE RIGHT SIGNALS

While costs are an important element in calculating a price – one you should never lose sight of – there are numerous other factors you need to take into account. For instance, your selling price can send an important signal to your customers. In the absence of other indicators, the price tells them if you are offering a cut-price deal or if you are at the top end of the market. To decide where your own price should lie demands knowledge of your target market and what the likely buyers are prepared to pay. This requires prior experience of the trade or accurate interpretation of your market research results.

In general terms, if you price slightly on the low side you will make more sales, but with a lower margin, and if you price slightly on the high side, you will make fewer sales but with a

DOS AND DON'TS OF PRICING

✓ Do put a realistic price on a product or service.

✓ Do make sure you include all the costs in your pricing calculations.

✓ Do take into account the true value of your own time.

✓ Do compare actual costs incurred on a job with the invoiced price.

✓ Do react quickly but thoughtfully to a competitor changing their prices.

✗ Don't forget to increase prices in line with inflation.

✗ Don't make the price hard to find in your sales literature.

✗ Don't price low just to get the work.

✗ Don't discount too much, too often.

✗ Don't think the customer is concerned only with the price.

greater margin, so the net profit will remain the same. The problem is, of course, knowing what constitutes a "high" or a "low" price; if you have existing competitors they will have already created price norms in the market. Finally, if you have one major customer, they may simply dictate what price they will pay, in which case your calculations will tell you if that is sufficient for your business to be viable.

CASE STUDY: Developing a Marketing Strategy

ONCE HE HAD left his job in the civil service, Michael began to set up his wine business, selling direct to consumers. His first task was to get his prices right. He had to be sure that he was including all his overheads, not overestimating likely sales, but at the same time establishing prices that would be attractive to buyers. His market was sensitive to price in that many of his potential customers would be very well aware of what their wine should cost. To coincide with the opening of his business, Michael also produced a press release, which he sent to his local newspapers; he backed this up with some targeted advertising in the same papers. He then considered incentives for customers to encourage them to introduce him to their friends; he would be relying on the personal touch and word of mouth to give him an edge in this highly competitive market.

Understanding Mark-ups and Margins

A mark-up is the amount added to the cost price to reach the selling price; a margin is the amount of profit you are making on an item. The calculation for a mark-up is:

$$\text{Mark-up (\%)} = \frac{(\text{Selling price} - \text{Cost price})}{\text{Cost price}} \times 100$$

The calculation for a margin is:

$$\text{Margin (\%)} = \frac{(\text{Selling price} - \text{Cost price})}{\text{Selling price}} \times 100$$

Mark-ups and margins vary from trade to trade, and in different parts of any supply chain. Learn the norms for your business; the only way to do this is to ask the trade, either through a trade association, or contacts. Beware of a common error: sometimes people say their mark-up is 200 per cent, meaning that they buy something for one price, and sell it for double that price. In fact, this is a mark-up of only 100 per cent.

Distribution and Pricing

How you distribute your product can make a great difference to your pricing. The main options for selling a product are selling direct

Money Saver

Be cautious about pricing your product on the assumption that you will be operating at full production all the time, for that is most unlikely. If you are working on your own, to work out a labour cost, charge at least what you would have to pay an employee to do the same work.

to the customer, using an agent on commission, or distributing through a wholesaler or retailer. Each method is appropriate to a particular trade, and you should know the mark-ups of the different distribution stages relevant to you so that you can work out your "end-user" price to see if it is competitive.

Some people, when starting a business, begrudge using wholesalers or retailers, because they feel they will take too much of the overall profit to be made on an item. However, selling direct to the customer takes both time and effort on promotion, neither of which is cheap. It might actually be better to sell indirectly through wholesalers or retailers, who already have the outlets and the customers.

Pricing for Wholesalers and Retailers

A straightforward way to price a product for wholesale or retail purposes is as follows:

**Selling price per unit =
Net cost price + Mark-up + VAT (if applicable)**

For example, if you buy an article for £4.65 net (without VAT added), and if the typical trade mark-up is 85 per cent, then the selling price would be calculated as follows:

£4.65 + 85% = £8.60

If you are VAT-registered and the article is liable for VAT, then you would add VAT on top of the total of £8.60.

There are several other points to consider:
■ You may consider rounding the price up or down to a figure (such as £8.50, or perhaps £8.99) that sounds more appealing to a customer.
■ Keep your prices in line with those of your competitors.
■ Check that your cash-flow forecast reflects your mark-ups, in terms of the relationship between the top "Sales" line and the "Stock/Raw Materials" line lower down. For example, if you are using a 100 per cent mark-up, then your "Stock/Raw Materials" line should be about half the value of the "Sales" line, or you will be destocking or overstocking gradually.

PRICING FOR MANUFACTURERS

If you are a manufacturer, a straightforward calculation to price a product is:

Selling price per unit =

(Cost of raw material + Direct labour + Overheads contribution) + Mark–up + VAT, where applicable

You can calculate the elements in this sum in the following way:

■ **COST OF RAW MATERIAL** This should be relatively easy to calculate per item, but do remember to allow for wastage.

■ **DIRECT LABOUR** This is the realistic cost of employing staff to make the units. Staff costs should include about one-third as much again on top of the wage to allow for National Insurance, paid holidays, and so on. If you are self-employed, do not be tempted to price your own labour costs cheaply – if you do, and you take on staff at a future date, you will either have to raise prices or take a drop in profits to cover the extra cost.

Price to achieve the maximum profit possible

■ **MARK-UP** To work this out, insert a known mark-up appropriate for your trade into the pricing equation (see opposite) to obtain your selling price; you can then make slight adjustments to the final price as necessary. The mark-up needs to provide a small surplus (say five to ten per cent) to provide funds for future expansion, new product development, or simply to save for any future contingencies.

■ **VAT** This is added only if your business is VAT-registered and if the product itself is VAT-rated (see pp. 179–81).

■ **OVERHEADS CONTRIBUTION** This considers the overheads (fixed costs) of the business, which obviously have to be supported by the production. To work out the overheads contribution per item, use the following calculation:

Overheads contribution =
$$\frac{\text{Total overheads}}{\text{Total production}}$$

An important point to note is that this calculation assumes that everything that is produced is subsequently sold.

CASE STUDY: Working Out the Unit Price

ELLEN IS self-employed, making children's garments. The raw materials cost £10 per unit (allowing for wastage), and each item takes one hour to make, so in a 40-hour week she might make 35 such items (allowing for downtime, time spent on administration, and so on). The labour cost is £200 – equivalent to what it would cost to pay an employee to do the job, plus one-third extra for paid holidays, sick leave, and so on. So the direct labour cost would be:

$$\frac{£200 + £66.67}{35} = £7.62 \text{ per unit}$$

Assume total overheads come to £8,000 a year, and total annual production is 1,680 items (for 48 weeks' production, allowing for some holidays). The overheads contribution is:

$$\frac{£8,000}{1,680} = £4.76 \text{ per unit}$$

Finally a mark-up is added of ten per cent. The selling price, therefore, is:

(£10 + £7.62 + £4.76) + 10% = £24.62

In this case, there is no need to add VAT. Ellen might choose to sell at more or less, depending on the competition and the market.

PRICING SERVICES

The pricing of services is usually based on hourly labour rates plus material costs. For consultancy or freelance work, this is usually called "fees plus expenses".

■ CALCULATING HOURLY LABOUR RATES

Hourly rate (+ VAT, where applicable) =

$$\frac{\text{(Total overheads including all wages)}}{\text{Total likely productive hours}} + \text{Mark-up}$$

First of all, find out the typical "going rate" for what you are planning to do. If you plan to employ anyone, allow an adequate hourly wage for them out of the amount you are planning to charge, making allowance for downtime and profit. Work out overheads and an appropriate mark-up. To calculate your productive hours, assume you (and any employees) will be productive (doing work for which you can actually charge) for, say, 75 per cent of the working week. The actual figure may be lower. Being productive for 75 per cent of the time means that in a typical 40-hour week you will only be charging for 30 hours, but having to pay your staff for 40. The remaining ten hours are absorbed in getting sales, doing paperwork, travelling, buying materials, and so on. Do the calculation, and insert that figure into your cash-flow forecast. If the cash-flow forecast figure looks good, and your labour rate is about that for the trade, that is a good start. If not, see what you can realistically adjust.

■ **MATERIALS** These are usually charged "at cost", but charging your customer the price you paid ignores the time you take to locate the materials, the cost of travel to collect them, materials held in stock, and so on. So most businesses define "at cost" as the retail price; they purchase the goods at trade or wholesale prices, giving themselves some margin.

CASE STUDY: Working Out an Hourly Rate

PAOLO AND GEORGE run a small car servicing and repair business as a partnership with no employees. Their overheads are £25,000 per year, and their basic working week is about 50 hours. They reckon they can do productive work for 40 hours (administration and cleaning taking up the balance of time). They take four weeks' holiday per year and, when possible, draw £15,000 a year each. The equation, assuming a ten per cent mark-up, would then be:

$$\frac{(£25,000 + £15,000 + £15,000)}{2 \times (40 \text{ hours} \times 48 \text{ weeks})} + 10\%$$

$$= £15.75 + \text{VAT}$$

The hourly rate is very dependent on them achieving a full 40-hour productive week with no time lost. In practice, they also make a useful profit on the spare parts being fitted.

CASE STUDY: Looking at Different Options for Charging

CAROLINE IS A graphic designer who wants to freelance. She plans to work on her own from home and to visit clients as necessary to get work and to discuss projects. She calculates the minimum hourly rate she must charge to provide an adequate "wage", and to cover any overheads she has. She needs to allow for time lost due to travelling, getting work, and administration. Any materials used she will charge at cost. She may be able to quote her hourly rate for some jobs, while in others she may be given a budget to work to or be asked to quote an overall price. Her difficulty in the latter situations would be estimating how long the job might take. She plans to keep a time log and, at the end of a fixed-price job, she will use it to calculate the actual hourly rate she achieved – this will help her with future estimates.

ESTIMATES AND QUOTATIONS

Service businesses usually operate by providing customers with an estimate (or quotation) which, if accepted by the customer, forms the basis of the contract between the two parties. An "estimate" is the approximate price for doing a job, but usually a buyer will ask for a "quotation" in writing. A quotation is a fixed price and, if agreed, is binding on both parties. You may be able to quote on a separate basis for each client, but always look at previous quotes to a client before submitting a new one so that you can keep the basics consistent.

MONEY SAVER

Avoid unnecessary friction with customers by advising them in advance if a price is likely to change (often prompted by the customer changing their specification). Since all quotations involve some guesswork, carefully record the actual time and materials you spend on fulfilling each contract. In this way your guesses should get more accurate with experience.

QUOTATION

If you have to do a large number of quotations, it can be useful to have a standard template so that you can fill in the relevant details. Always put the date on the quotation, and make clear for how long it is valid. Be clear about exactly what is covered in the quotation, and include your payment terms.

Quantity and specification are described in detail

Length of time for which quote is valid is included

Payment terms are made clear

Secure Grilles

10 Sellers Lane
Any City AC1 1ZZ
Tel: 098-765 4321

Mrs S. Nixon, Manager
Excellent Products Ltd
Unit 3, Industrial Estate
Any Town BZ25 1ZZ

21 June 2001

Dear Mrs Nixon

WINDOW GRILLES – QUOTATION

Thank you for taking the time to meet me yesterday. I now have pleasure in providing you with a quote to supply and fit window security grilles for your factory unit.

QUANTITY	Four windows, all to the rear of the premises.
SPECIFICATION	Mild steel expanded mesh as per sample left with you. Grilles to be attached to window surrounds by one-way security screws.
PRICE	£623.00 + VAT. This quotation is valid for 30 days.
TERMS	Payment is due 30 days from date of invoice.
GUARANTEE	We guarantee our workmanship and materials for 12 months.

If you have any questions please do not hesitate to call me. I look forward to hearing from you in the near future.

Yours sincerely
Paul Wilson
Sales Manager

Partners: P. Wilson, J. Smith

Different Methods of Advertising

You can have a desirable product or service at an attractive price, but if nobody knows about it, it is unlikely to sell. There are many ways of advertising to find customers, and even a small business should aim to use a combination of these. Some advertising methods are more costly than others, while some are more effective. Cost and effect are not always clearly related.

The function of advertising is to arouse interest in specific readers and to encourage them to take the next step (to visit you, phone you, or buy your product). With most advertising you are trying to target the message at the person who can make the buying decision. It is therefore essential to choose the best medium for your message. To target your advertising, look back at your market research to help you ascertain who your customers are, where they live or work, what they like, what makes them different. This might help you to form a picture of the places and publications in which they are likely to notice advertising.

Your advertising needs to be part of a campaign. People tend to forget most single advertisements almost as soon as they have seen them, unless they happen to have a need for the product or service at the time they see the advertisement. A successful advertising campaign requires regular advertising. You need not take large advertisements, in fact a little and often is likely to give a better result.

As with any endeavour that will take time, money, and effort, you need to formulate a plan. This should set simple goals (such as an increase in sales of ten per cent within six months), a budget, likely timescales, and a means of monitoring the success of the plan. The clearer you are about your goals at the outset, the more likely you are to be able to measure your success and improve upon your campaign in the future.

COMMON ERRORS WITH ADVERTISING

1 Assuming one big advertisement is all that is necessary.

2 Placing an advertisement in response to pressure from advertising salespeople.

3 Advertising in the wrong place (or at the wrong time).

4 Advertising without a clear idea as to the objective.

5 Using your business name for the advertisement's headline.

6 Designing an advertisement that promotes image, then expecting a response.

7 Placing an advertisement too hastily, and not as part of an overall plan.

8 Omitting a clear call for action at the end of an advertisement.

9 Allowing too small a budget for advertising.

10 Continuing to place advertisements without monitoring the results.

ADVERTISING IN A NEWSPAPER, MAGAZINE, OR DIRECTORY

Before placing an advert in a publication, check to see if similar firms are advertising. If not, check again whether the publication will reach your target market. Directories can be a good place for small businesses to advertise, as long as the directory is one your target customers are likely to use. Many trades have their own directory. Ask businesses (not direct rivals) already advertising in a directory if they get much response from their entry. Some directory entries are simply a listing of the business name and address; if there is space for a comment, give it as much thought as you would for any other advertisement. Most directories are annual, so try to be sure your details will not change during the life of the directory.

Choosing an Advertising Method

Method	Cost	Advantages	Disadvantages
Direct Mailshot Letter	Low	■ Targeted audience ■ High response rate (2–5 per cent)	■ Time-consuming to locate or produce a good mailing list
Small Poster	Low	■ Large readership ■ Long life	■ Limited locations ■ Message must be short to make an immediate impact
Letterbox Leaflet	Low	■ Can be part-targeted	■ Low response rate ■ Post office distribution is most effective but increases the cost
Internet Web Site	Low/ Medium	■ Potentially huge audience ■ Full colour, sound, and some animation possible	■ Difficult to stand out in the crowd
Directories	Low/ Medium	■ Advert life is one year ■ Allows comparison with competitors ■ May have wide circulation	■ Can only make changes annually
Direct Mailshot Leaflet	Low/ Medium	■ Targeted audience	■ Response rate is variable ■ Time-consuming (but less so than direct mailshot letter)
Advert in Local Paper	Medium	■ Local audience ■ Can repeat often ■ Supporting editorial is possible	■ Readership much larger than your target market
Advert in Trade Publication	Medium/ High	■ Targeted ■ Editorial often possible ■ Publication can have long life	■ If publication is relevant, none, except price
Advert on Local Radio	High	■ Wide audience	■ Advert time very brief, so needs repeating frequently
Advert in National Magazine	High	■ National audience ■ Colour may be available	■ Editorial unlikely ■ Need to book space months ahead

To place an advert, check the advertising rates. For classified advertisements, rates will usually be quoted as cost per word or line, while display advertisements are usually quoted as cost per single column centimetre (scc) – a space one column wide and one centimetre deep. Larger display adverts are also quoted in terms of one-eighth, one-quarter, a half- or a full page. Check the deadline for submitting your advertisement. Ask for a rate card, which will give all this information plus details of the circulation of the publication. If you are booking an advert, send in a press release at the same time, to try to obtain extra coverage in the editorial (see pp. 96–7). It is often more effective to take out two or more different adverts in the same issue than one long one.

Pᴜᴛᴛɪɴɢ Tᴏɢᴇᴛʜᴇʀ ᴀɴ Aᴅᴠᴇʀᴛ

First, think about the content of your advert. It is tempting to try to address all readers – this is a scattershot approach and is rarely effective.

Sᴀᴍᴘʟᴇ Dɪsᴘʟᴀʏ Aᴅᴠᴇʀᴛɪsᴇᴍᴇɴᴛ

This eye-catching advert focuses on particular items for sale. An incentive is offered to encourage a prompt response, and a 24-hour phone number is given.

Good-quality photograph is used both to attract attention and to show items for sale

Call for action by offering an incentive

Design is simple, with no clutter to detract from the basic message

Headline promises a benefit and may therefore catch the attention of more prospective customers than a specific heading such as "Garden Furniture"

Principal objective is to stimulate customers to request a brochure or visit the web site

ENJOY THE OUTDOORS
Top brands of garden furniture in teak, cast iron, aluminium, etc
■ Wɪᴅᴇ Rᴀɴɢᴇ, Aʟʟ ɪɴ Sᴛᴏᴄᴋ ■

For your free colour brochure call our
24–HOUR ORDERLINE
012-345 6789
or visit our web site at **www. ... .com**

John Smith Garden Centre
Rose Street, Any Town

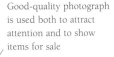
10% OFF ORDERS PLACED BY 31 MAY

Contact details are provided

Instead, address the advert to a specific section of the readership who will at least consider your product or service. Your advert must be honest, and never misleading; you must avoid applying false trade descriptions to goods or services, and you must be able to prove any performance claims you make.

Avoid cluttering the advert in an attempt to squeeze in all sorts of information about different products. To encourage potential buyers to take the next step, you could try putting a closing date or using words demanding action. If you are giving a phone number in the advert, ensure someone will be there to answer it.

Keep your advertisements simple and to the point

Designing adverts demands time, thought, creativity, and experience. It is all too easy to get it wrong and produce an advert that costs money but produces little result. Look for eye-catching adverts in previous issues of the publication in which you plan to advertise, and try to analyze what makes them successful. If you are using a classified advert, it needs a catchy heading. If you are placing a display advert, a good photograph or image is often more informative and enticing than text.

Many new businesses give prominence in an advert to their company name. However, unless the name is very descriptive, that is largely wasted space; an unknown name has little impact or meaning. Building brand or company name awareness takes a very big advertising budget – usually out of the question for a new small business. However, if your business represents or sells a well-known brand name, it may be useful to give that prominence (check first with the company concerned – they may even pay a portion of the cost of the advert).

An effective style of display advert is one that looks and reads like a news item or feature article. In most cases it will be necessary to have the words "Paid Advertisement" at the top. If written skilfully, it can be worthwhile, but it must not be misleading. This type of advert tends to cost more than others, as it is generally larger.

LEAFLETS AND BROCHURES

The purpose of a leaflet (also a pamphlet or brochure) is to convey a message in a lasting form. Leaflets can also carry a much longer, more detailed, message than an advert, and can be distributed to a targeted group of people or sent out in response to an enquiry. Distribution of leaflets is very dependent upon your product or service and your likely customers. The most obvious way is to post them through letterboxes yourself or you could use the post office, who will distribute them along with the post for a fee. An alternative is to pay to have them inserted loose in a newspaper or magazine. This is particularly popular in trade publications. If your target market is local consumers, your local newsagent may, for a small charge, include them with the paper round. Finally, you could hand them out at special events that attract your type of customer (for which you should have the organizer's permission), or distribute them in the street (for which you may need the local council's permission). To design a leaflet or brochure, consider the following:

■ SIZE This will be determined by the amount of information you need to convey, the

TIME SAVER

Producing an effective, quality advertisement takes time and expertise. It may save you time (and ultimately produce a more effective advertisement) if you use a designer to help you. Look at adverts the designer has produced in the past, to form an idea of their work. Provide a detailed written brief as to your requirements, and ask about his or her likely charges.

intended method of distribution (for example, does your leaflet need to fit into an envelope?), and the amount you can afford to spend. Your leaflet is best kept to a standard size, and can be flat or folded, printed on one or both sides.

■ Colour A full-colour leaflet is expensive. It is, however, justified if the product or service you are offering is itself expensive, or needs colour to show its features fully (for example, a wallpaper leaflet would be pointless in black and white), or if it needs to be in colour to compete with a rival's full-colour leaflet. Note that you need full-colour printing only if you are incorporating colour photographs. If full colour is not essential, great effect can be achieved by using two colours for a much lower price. Be careful of printing black on brightly coloured paper, as this is often used to advertise cheap products or services. If you have a computer and good-quality colour printer you can create

Sample Leaflet
This sample leaflet to promote garden furniture in the spring attracts attention by offering a benefit. Information follows about the range of furniture available, prices, and contact details.

Introductory comment clearly explains what is on offer

Main part elaborates on the offer. Enough information is given to arouse interest, and prices are given

Call for action by offering an incentive

Business name and contact details are clearly stated, but not unnecessarily prominent

Headline promises a benefit and may therefore catch the attention of more prospective customers than a specific heading such as "Garden Furniture"

Professional photograph is included

Text is arranged in well-spaced blocks so that it is easy to read

Additional items in range are mentioned, but should only be included if there is space

Business slogan is an optional extra

MAKE THE MOST OF SUMMER
WITH YOUR FAMILY AND FRIENDS

GARDEN FURNITURE – HUGE STOCK

We can now offer a complete choice of attractive, comfortable, and yet affordable garden furniture in pine, aluminium or plastic. Elegantly designed and carefully made to be enjoyed and admired. Chairs from £19.95, tables from £49.95.

SPECIAL OFFER 20% DISCOUNT
If you bring this leaflet and buy at least one table and four chairs before 31 May.

We also stock a full range of pots, plants, potting mixes, tools, seed, hoses, fertilizers, gravel, seedling trays, sprays, garden sheds ....

John Smith Garden Centre
Rose Street, Any Town Tel: 012-345 6789
www. .... .com

For the Greenest of Gardens

your own leaflets. This is best done only when the numbers of leaflets needed are small – probably 50 or fewer.

■ **MATERIAL** Look at several weights of paper or card before making your decision. A glossy or semi-matt coated finish and thicker paper are more expensive, but give a high-quality impression.

■ **CONTENT** This will obviously vary hugely, but there are a number of guidelines you can follow in most cases. Think of a catchy heading to focus the reader's mind. It can either be descriptive ("Garden Furniture"), questioning ("Need Smart New Garden Furniture?"), assertive ("Garden Furniture Now in Stock"), or indicating a benefit ("Make the Most of Summer with Your Family and Friends"). Add some text explaining the heading; make it as short as possible, and keep it interesting. You are producing the leaflet because you want it to trigger some reaction. The end of the leaflet should therefore urge the reader to do something, such as contact you, so your address, e-mail address (if you have one), and phone number should be given clearly. A simple reply coupon can be useful in some cases. Include a map if you are not near to a town centre or are hard to find.

■ **DESIGN** For a leaflet to achieve maximum effect, the design must be professional. It is a good idea to employ a designer to help.

■ **FOLDER** This is a specialized style of leaflet, suitable where you are dealing with a small customer base (under 100 or so), and the product or service you are supplying is either complex or changing. The idea is to print a smart folder of lightweight card, usually slightly larger than A4 in size. Into this folder you can slip sheets of information, possibly an introductory letter, and, where applicable, photographs. The folder gives impact to your presentation while maintaining maximum flexibility by allowing you to add to or change the information sheets within it.

DIRECT MAIL

Consisting of a letter, a leaflet, or (more usually) both, direct mail is targeted at consumers or business customers. Its strength, or weakness, lies in the quality of the mailing list on which the mailshot is based. Direct mail is particularly useful for selling to existing customers whose details you already have on record, and can be used to notify them of new products and services, price changes, special offers, or anything else that might encourage them to place an order. You might also use it as a reminder for customers who order regularly.

POSTERS

A small business is more likely to use small posters aimed at the local market rather than large posters on billboards. The best use of posters is to advertise a specific event, such as a sale, or an opening. Usually permission should be sought from the local authority before putting up posters. Decide the sites you would like to use, then design the poster accordingly. If the people who will read the poster are on foot, the design can be slightly more detailed. For passing cars, the text needs to be brief and readable from a distance.

INTERNET

Having a presence on the internet with a web site is an important marketing tool for many businesses. It is vital to recognize that your web site is an advertisement like any other advertisement and should therefore be designed with that in mind. In addition to having your own web site, you might consider paying to have an advert on someone else's web pages, especially their home page; the effectiveness of such advertising is uncertain, but it may be worth experimenting if you have the budget. See pp. 101–5 for more details on web sites.

LOCAL RADIO

Commercial radio can be an effective advertising medium for a wide range of local consumer and business-orientated products or services, and is a suitable place for small businesses to advertise. Start by speaking to the radio station's advertising manager and ask which times of day are best for your particular business to advertise.

Costs are based on airtime, and you need to add about ten per cent to cover the production costs of making the commercial. Research shows that the length of the commercial makes little difference to its impact, so choose as short a slot as your message requires.

Most local radio stations can help you to produce the commercial in their studios. A common mistake is to try to squeeze in too many words: in a 30-second slot with a brief jingle, there is only time for about 100 words, spoken quickly. Research has shown that commercials with dialogue between two or more people achieve higher impact than a single voice. The radio station will also have free library music that you can use. Ask for a demo advert, so you can hear in advance how your advert will sound.

MONITORING RESULTS

Few businesses, large or small, make enough of an attempt to monitor the results of their advertising. In fact this is crucial to testing and refining your advertising strategy. There are basically three direct ways and one indirect way in which you can monitor responses.

The simplest way is to ask the customer who phones or calls in person how they heard about your business. Alternatively, if a customer is replying by post, you can add an extra line (such as a name or a room number) to the address you give; as you receive replies you can detect the source of the enquiry. You can also see which adverts have produced a response if the reader is invited to bring or send a coupon or form from the advert; this is particularly useful in a retail context. Finally, the indirect method is to see if your overall sales change, all other factors remaining the same; in practice this is rarely the case over a long timespan, but you may be able to detect a trend.

TIPS FOR YOUR PRESS RELEASE

1. Try to tie in your news with some bigger event or story that the publication is already running.

2. Submit the press release well before the publishing deadline.

3. Keep the press release short (ideally under a page).

4. Write to catch the eye and hold the reader's interest.

5. Put the most important aspect in the first paragraph, since any editing is usually done from the bottom up.

6. If possible, include a good photograph or two with the press release.

7. Follow up the press release by phoning the appropriate editorial department – this is not always a popular strategy with journalists, but it can work and may give you some feedback, too.

Public Relations

This is a term for all the activities aimed at communicating an image and message about your business and products into the marketplace. If you can afford it, you can employ a PR consultant. For most small businesses, however, the main method of PR is to compose a press release and send it to relevant publications whenever you have a story that is newsworthy. The publication may then use the text from your press release to form a story or feature. Since the story is in the main body of the publication, this is not perceived as advertising, and often appears authoritative and therefore effective. Remember that the publication may or may not use your news item, they may choose to use it days or weeks later, and they may write the article in their own words and with their own bias. Trade publications are more likely to use your press release than the consumer press, and tend to be less ruthless in their treatment of stories.

Write your press release carefully, adjusting it as necessary to the tone or emphasis of the publication. Avoid superlatives or making suspect claims. Journalists prefer to have advance warning of events, but if you do not want premature publicity you can request the publication not to print anything on the subject until the date shown. Whenever possible, include clear, sharp photographs or transparencies, preferably taken by a professional photographer. Some local papers prefer to send their own photographer, so ask before you incur unnecessary expense. If you are sending a photograph, attach a clear description of what it shows (especially the names of people).

PRESS RELEASE

Keep your press release short, factual, and to the point, but ensure that it includes all the information a journalist is likely to need to write an article.

Headed notepaper is used, with contact details

Since press release ties in with a specific event, it indicates the earliest date for publication

Subject of press release is clearly indicated in heading

Start with the newsworthy event, then put it into context

Quotations and comments are included from relevant people

Indicates that photographs are included

Direct contact details

SPEEDY RALLY CONVERSIONS
8 Main Road, Old Town

PRESS RELEASE
NOT FOR PUBLICATION OR BROADCAST BEFORE 2 MAY

LAUNCH OF NEW RALLY CAR BUSINESS

At a short ceremony in the old town today, Bobby Millar, the rally driver, launched a new rally car preparation business called Speedy Rally Conversions.

SRC, located at 8 Main Road, will take high-performance road cars and prepare them to full rally standards. This will entail completely stripping down the original vehicle, strengthening the body shell, and adding a protective roll cage, then carefully fitting the new, highly tuned engine, transmission, and running gear.

Jim Smith, 42, the proprietor of the new business and a former amateur rally driver, said: "At present many rally drivers have difficulty in finding the right expertise in this part of the country. I hope SRC will meet their needs."

Bobby Millar, 32, who now lives in the town, said: "I need my rally cars to be prepared to the highest standards and I am confident that SRC are the very people to do this for me in the future."

PHOTOGRAPH attached

FOR MORE INFORMATION:
Contact: Jim Smith
Tel: 098-765 4321

SALES AND PROMOTION

Selling your products or services is one of the most crucial aspects of running a small business. Advertising and PR let potential customers know that you exist and encourage sales, but there is no substitute for excellent promotional and selling skills when it comes to making a sale. This chapter covers a variety of promotional techniques, different selling forums, ways of negotiating, and how to build a good working relationship with your customers over the long term.

There are almost as many ways of promoting sales as there are business ideas. Promotion differs from advertising in that it is much more proactive; it aims to stimulate the buyer into making a purchase at once. Although often cheaper than conventional advertising, promotion still costs money. In recent decades, consumers have been subjected to a flood of promotional gimmicks, so really effective promotion has become increasingly difficult, especially on a small budget. Trade buyers are not quite so saturated, but are perhaps more cynical. Promotions are also time-consuming. When you do a promotion, monitor its progress and weigh up if the resulting sales justify the time spent.

It is important to note that how you promote sales can depend on the circumstances and the timing; for the best results you need to focus

Keep trying out innovative forms of promotion to appeal to new and existing customers

on achieving a particular objective. If you wish to counter a competitor who has dramatically reduced their prices, for example, then you can either engage in a price war (not usually a good idea) or start a promotion that stresses why your product or service merits the apparently higher price. A different approach would be required to increase market share; in this case you would need to concentrate on the best ways of enticing customers away from your rivals. If you are promoting a new and innovative product, you may need to concentrate on drawing attention to the nature and purpose of the innovations.

Many of the most successful methods of promotion are covered in the chart opposite. Exhibitions and seminars are among the most useful and productive promotional means for small businesses and are covered in more detail on p. 100.

CASE STUDY: Choosing Promotional Methods

ANDY HAD RETIRED from the military. He was a talented painter, specializing in military subjects, and now wanted to make a living using this skill. His initial market research indicated there was a niche market, which would be best met by a mix of prints and commissioned originals. His target market would be not only serving and retired members of the armed forces, but also members of the public with an interest in military matters. There was additional interest from overseas. He therefore decided to create a web site offering on-line ordering, and to try to make sales in person at military events that were open to the public. He also planned to create a mailing list of customers who might be interested in purchasing prints on an occasional basis.

PROMOTIONAL TECHNIQUES

TECHNIQUE	DEFINITION	POINTS TO CONSIDER
MAILSHOT	A personalized letter or a leaflet is sent to a customer introducing a special offer	■ Useful for both consumer and trade customers ■ Cost is average compared to other methods, but depends on complexity of design ■ Response rate variable and unpredictable
SAMPLE	A sample of a product is sent to an individual	■ Effective when sent to someone with major buying power in an organization, or to someone who influences buyers, such as the editor of a magazine ■ Follow up with a phone call a week or so after sending
FREE TRIAL	The customer tries out a product before buying or as an incentive to buy	■ Most suitable for high-value once-purchase items, which the customer tries for a set period of time, or for low-value repeat-purchase items, such as consumables ■ Can be very effective with target market
COMPETITIONS/ RAFFLES	A raffle is organized with prizes of the products to be promoted	■ Requires legal advice to comply with regulations governing raffles, and local authority permission to sell the tickets ■ Prize must be suitably attractive (or expensive) for people to enter the raffle
IN-STORE DEMOS	A manufacturer or importer organizes a demonstration of a product in a store	■ Store is usually carrying the product, so the demo often results in immediate sales ■ Demo needs to be carried out with enthusiasm
OPEN DAYS	An office, workshop, or studio is opened to the public	■ A lot of organization is needed to make the day successful ■ Need to put on special displays to interest visitors ■ Event must be publicized well in advance ■ Check you are covered by insurance for visitors
VIDEO/CD	Information about a product is made available on a video or as video clips on a CD-ROM	■ Ideal for conveying a complex message or to demonstrate how a product works ■ A CD-ROM could have an interactive element and a Frequently Asked Questions (FAQ) section ■ Expensive to produce and to alter
FASHION SHOW	Used in the fashion and accessory industry, a show is put on to display new products	■ Requires considerable time, skill, and money to stage an impressive show with the right venue, experienced models, and good-quality sound and lighting ■ A good means of influencing trade and public buyers

Exhibitions and Seminars

For non-retail businesses, sales generally have to be made on a one-to-one basis, which is very time-consuming. However, there are two special opportunities where such a business can meet potential customers *en masse* – at an exhibition and at a seminar. In the case of an exhibition, your business has to show its wares alongside competitors, while in the case of a seminar you are the organizer and usually the only business giving a presentation.

EXHIBITIONS

These include consumer shows and trade fairs, and have increased hugely in importance. For non-retail businesses they can provide regional, national, and even international exposure. Do not pitch your expectations too high – many new exhibitors are disappointed with the

MONEY SAVER

At most exhibition venues, the provision of electric power or any furnishings can be disproportionately expensive in relation to the cost of the stand space, so take your own furnishings, and try to avoid using electric power (unless the venue is so dark you need stand lighting).

results of their initial showings. This is usually due to inexperience, although if you are getting consistent feedback about the viability or otherwise of your product or service, ensure that you listen to it. Approach all exhibitions with an open mind and be ready to learn from other exhibitors and from your own mistakes.

Making the most of exhibiting requires a great deal of preparation, an adequate budget, and hard work before, during, and after the event. Because exhibiting can be time-consuming and expensive, the decision to participate should not be taken lightly.

During the show you and your staff need to pace yourselves, especially if the show lasts for several days. Take time out to rest, eat, and sit down whenever you can. Depending on the industry, the selling opportunities vary. At some exhibitions you make sales on the spot; at others you may just take orders; at others the main purpose is to make buyers aware of what you have to offer. Be sure in advance what you need to offer, and be ready as appropriate with supplies of stock, the facility to handle cash, cheques, or credit card transactions safely, or order forms for taking names and addresses so you can follow up after the show. Each evening you should have a review of how the day went and make whatever adjustments are necessary ready for the following day.

After the show you need to allow time to follow up the sales leads you have made, and to catch up with all the other routine paperwork that will have been mounting up in your office while you were away.

PREPARING FOR AN EXHIBITION

1 Visit a number of similar exhibitions and talk to the organizers.

2 Decide which show or shows are the most appropriate for you.

3 Read the small print of the exhibition terms and conditions.

4 Design your stand or stands to be eye-catching and sufficiently interesting to keep someone from just walking past.

5 Organize what you will display on your stand, and leaflets to give away.

6 Decide on any pre-exhibition supporting publicity to encourage people to come and visit your stand.

7 Work out staffing rosters and book local accommodation.

8 If necessary, train staff in how to sell effectively from the stand.

SEMINARS, TALKS, AND DEMONSTRATIONS

These are events organized by you where you invite carefully chosen people who are likely buyers of your product or service. The key is to get the right audience. Once you have your captive audience, you can give them your sales pitch. Such events can be very useful for many different businesses, including both service-based and manufacturing concerns.

If you are selling to trade buyers, you may be able to tag your seminar on to some other event (such as a trade association or chamber of commerce meeting). If not, to get the buyers to come, you need to make the occasion sound interesting and appealing – offering lunch or drinks at a venue such as a local hotel may help to encourage their appearance.

It is vital to ensure that the presentation itself is entertaining and of a high standard. Whether you are doing the presentation yourself, or hiring a professional speaker, take the time to prepare high-quality visual aids (such as slides,

HOLDING A SEMINAR

In this small seminar, visuals are used in order to show the key features of a product. The restricted number of participants means that the salesperson can take the time to answer individual questions in detail.

a video, or a multimedia presentation), samples on display, and leaflets for people to take away. Rehearse at least once at the venue to get used to the conditions, time the presentation, and to iron out any technical hitches.

Internet and e-commerce

There is little doubt that an increasing amount of business is being done over the internet. The word "e-commerce" simply means carrying out business transactions over the internet. The relationship between customers and suppliers is being radically affected by the internet; customers can place orders electronically and then track the progress of the goods right into their warehouses or homes. The rapidly expanding internet market presents opportunities and threats to small business. On the one hand, it can give a small business a window to the world for its products (and services to a lesser degree) and a presence equivalent to its larger rivals; on the other hand, it poses the challenge of competition from far and wide.

BUSINESS USES OF THE INTERNET

The internet is an exciting and potentially highly beneficial tool for businesses. Nevertheless, it is important to consider what you want to achieve through this new medium, just as it is for any other new venture. Typical tasks carried out by small businesses through their web sites include:

■ Sending and receiving e-mails (both internally and externally).

DOS AND DON'TS OF WEB SITES

✓ Do make it clear what you do and what you are offering on the home page.

✓ Do include some background information on your business on your site.

✓ Do have a "return to home" button on each page.

✓ Do provide an opportunity for feedback by e-mail or telephone.

✓ Do give your full postal address, to establish credibility.

✓ Do ensure your site is registered with all major search engines.

✓ Do offer added value on the site, with useful information and free downloads.

✗ Don't include too many photos on your opening page, as they slow it down.

✗ Don't have too many layers requiring a great deal of mouse-clicking.

✗ Don't insist on registration simply to get on to your site.

✗ Don't be anonymous – provide contact names and e-mail addresses.

■ Sourcing services, stock, raw materials, and consumables (the internet throws your buying net wider).

■ Publishing on-line sales catalogues (which have the big advantage that they can be updated easily and quickly and can also be used for publicizing special offers).

■ Selling goods on-line.

■ Providing technical support and back-up (this reduces time-consuming phone calls from customers with problems, and provides customers with a more efficient service).

■ Carrying out market research (there is a huge amount of information available on-line, much of it free).

■ Checking out competitors (the amount of information available can be stunning and revealing).

■ Exchanging order information with customers and suppliers (this reduces the amount of paperwork and provides trading partners with increased information about the other party, such as stock levels and despatch details).

■ Managing a bank account (including paying business bills by internet banking).

WHICH BUSINESSES CAN BENEFIT FROM USING THE INTERNET?

All businesses will benefit from at least some of the business uses of the internet that are listed above. While many business web sites simply provide information, there is a huge growth in the number of businesses who are selling their products and services on-line. The internet is changing fast and maturing in the ways in which it is used, but at present the main growth area is in business-to-business trading and the slowest rate of growth is in businesses providing services in person to consumers. A service-based company might nevertheless use a web site primarily to promote their business.

To some extent, selling via the internet is like selling through a catalogue that can be constantly updated, and permits the customer to place orders electronically (and, in some

RESEARCHING WEB-SITE DESIGN

Look at a variety of web sites set up by large and small businesses. Note features that you like and that make the site easier to use. Explore other pages apart from the home page to understand the site layout.

A "Help" guide is useful where a site contains numerous pages, or to assist with an interactive process such as selling

Name of business is a prominent feature of the web page

Navigation buttons make it easy for the user to find information and connect to other pages on the site

A "Search" feature is useful on large sites or those containing complex information

Users can choose whether to access more information

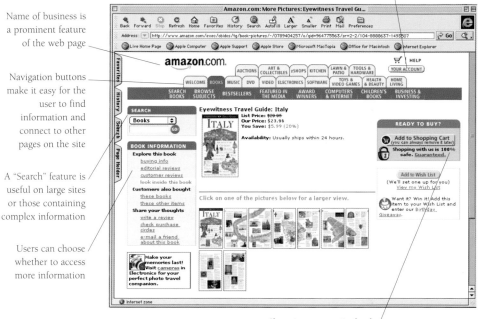

Shopping process is clearly indicated, and security aspects are emphasized

specialized cases, such as software and music, to take delivery electronically as well). As always, the big question is: Will a professionally designed web site generate enough on-line business to justify its cost and the time taken to set it up? The setting-up costs are dropping dramatically, thereby reducing the risk. At the same time, with secure credit card transactions now possible, customers are more prepared to buy on-line. A key factor is how committed your business is to moving in this direction.

CREATING A GOOD WEB SITE

If you have seen other business web sites, you will certainly know that the quality and ease of use of different sites varies considerably. Some

are straightforward to use, while others are far less so. Visit a variety of web sites and note features that appeal to you and that you find easy to use. Analyze how the site is structured and the usefulness of the various links. As with the design of any advertisement, keep in mind your target market and their needs, as well as your own e-commerce objectives.

Your opening home page should load quickly, have your trading title clearly visible, and make a firm and direct statement as to who you are and what you do, so that the visitor knows if the site is relevant to them. You want not only to attract the right visitors, but also to keep them interested enough to browse your other pages. A home page benefits from buttons that give clear options for moving around the site and locating further information, and ideally does not require scrolling down.

Promotion of your web site is as important an activity as the creation of the web site itself. Merely creating a web site is unlikely to generate sufficient visitors. Right from the start you should consider the keywords for the search engines to find. Look at rival sites to see what keywords they use. Include also common misspellings of your keywords. Ensure your new web site is registered with all major search engines. Once it is up and running, be sure to promote the site through any other advertising you do, giving your web site address on all your correspondence and literature, business cards, products, and even your van sides, where appropriate. There is also proactive marketing of your site, in which you look for other sites that relate to yours and suggest a hypertext link directly to your site. This is a time-consuming but potentially very worthwhile process.

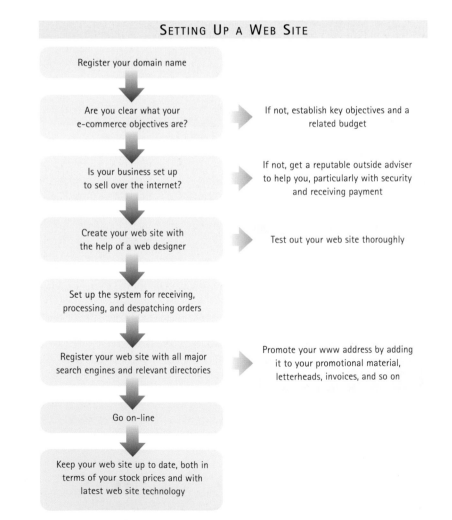

SETTING UP A WEB SITE

Register your domain name

Are you clear what your e-commerce objectives are? → If not, establish key objectives and a related budget

Is your business set up to sell over the internet? → If not, get a reputable outside adviser to help you, particularly with security and receiving payment

Create your web site with the help of a web designer → Test out your web site thoroughly

Set up the system for receiving, processing, and despatching orders

Register your web site with all major search engines and relevant directories → Promote your www address by adding it to your promotional material, letterheads, invoices, and so on

Go on-line

Keep your web site up to date, both in terms of your stock prices and with latest web site technology

Finally, for many businesses, the internet offers a new sales channel, but you should use it as an additional means rather than neglecting traditional channels in its favour.

SELLING ON-LINE

If one of your objectives is to sell on-line, there are several issues you need to consider. The first of these is how to have secure credit card or debit card transactions. This is relatively easy, but requires specialist knowledge to set up properly. Another issue is that your business should be structured to process these new orders and to take care of the extra workload associated with the many e-mails (some of them junk ones) that are inevitable. It is difficult to anticipate likely demand in terms of orders, and in fact initial demand is likely to be slow, but you should be fully prepared to react as the situation develops. If you are selling a product, it is vital not to run out of stock.

UPDATING YOUR WEB SITE

After putting a great deal of thought, effort, and money into creating your new web site, you need to keep it up to date to maintain its effectiveness. Having out-of-date information on a web site reflects badly on the business concerned. For certain businesses, such as estate agents, having out-of-date information makes the site useless. People will not visit a poor site twice. If you do not have the time or resources to dedicate to updating detailed information on your web site, then keep it simple; the site could act as an initial point of contact, telling visitors how to contact your business through other means.

In addition to keeping the content of your site current, you need to monitor the major search engines to ensure they not only locate your site, but give it a high ranking when the right keywords are typed in. From time to time arrange to have your site checked over from a technological point of view, to ensure that it remains compatible and easy to use with the latest browser software.

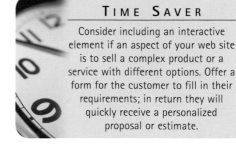

Face-to-face Selling

With the exception of former sales staff, most people who start their own business have not had to sell to others before, and may feel somewhat daunted by the idea. There are many basic selling techniques that can easily be learned and, when put into practice, will result in good sales. Even the most reluctant salesperson can get a real buzz out of making a sale, particularly where clinching the sale depended on their sales technique.

There is a saying that "customers buy benefits, not goods or services". Once you have understood that basic concept, the whole art of selling begins to make more sense. What the saying actually means is best illustrated by an example. Two soccer fans may buy a video recorder because they want the benefit of being able to replay their favourite matches. If there were some better way they could do that, they might not buy a video recorder. In other words, it is not really the video recorder they need and are buying, but the benefit it gives them.

Your starting point is to know your product inside out, and to be fully aware of all its potential benefits to buyers.

FINDING NEW CUSTOMERS

When you start up in business you may have a few key customers in mind, but will need to find more to expand. As the business grows, it is important to keep building on your list of customers. In some cases, potential customers will find you as a result of a recommendation from a satisfied customer, and they are very likely to become buyers. Usually, however, you will have to find customers yourself. This can be by direct means; for example, if you are a service business, you can find potential customers from listings in trade directories then contact them directly. You can also find customers, both other businesses and the general public, by indirect means, such as through your advertisements or other promotions.

Getting an Appointment

To get an appointment with a prospective customer (or "prospect"), the best strategy is first to find out the name of the person who has the buying authority. You can usually do this by phoning the business concerned, explaining that you wish to write to the buyer, and asking for the buyer's name. Occasionally, you will be put directly through to the buyer even though this is not what you asked for, so be prepared for this eventuality. Once you have the buyer's name, write a letter enclosing relevant sales information. In the letter, state that you will phone to discuss the contents in about a week's time (if you ask the buyer to call you, you will rarely get a response).

About a week or so after sending the letter, telephone the buyer to make an appointment. Be positive and friendly, but not pushy. Some buyers will be keen to see you, others will refuse directly, others may simply avoid you. Try a few times, and if you are not successful then try another business, and make a note to approach the original buyer again in a few months to see if their needs have changed.

Preparation

It is vital to prepare carefully for any face-to-face selling appointment. Make sure you are familiar with background information concerning the person and the business you are going to see, and that you have thought through their possible needs and requirements.

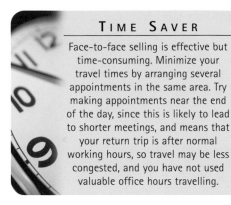

Gather together your sales material and ensure that you know it thoroughly. Sales material is a key element of face-to-face selling. It consists of samples, brochures, your business cards, order forms, and possibly a calculator or laptop computer if you need to come up with estimates or quotations on the spot. If you do not have a good brochure and it is not possible to carry samples due to their size, an effective substitute is good-quality photographs neatly presented in a folder or album. Letters of commendation, relevant newspaper cuttings, certificates of technical competence, and so on, can also be useful when presenting your case. Have your price lists to hand and ensure that you know your bottom price – the price below which you are not prepared to go.

If dealing with a buyer from another culture, research the norms and etiquette in their culture for selling and negotiation. Their way of doing business may be very different to yours, so you need to build this into your plan. There are numerous books dealing with this subject. An alternative is to use an agent or other representative who is familiar with that culture and who can advise you on your best approach.

Opening the Sale

Arrive at your appointment in good time. To open any sale (see also pp. 108–9), use the same friendly gestures as you would on meeting anyone new for the first time. Smile, make direct eye contact, and start with a genuine "hello" and a warm handshake. Hand over your business card if you have not met before and, if appropriate, ask for theirs.

Maintain open, non-threatening body language and a positive attitude throughout the meeting. Try to sit close enough to be friendly, but not so close as to be overfamiliar – respect personal space (and note that perceptions of personal space vary from culture to culture). It is conventional to discuss briefly topics that are not controversial, such as your journey, before getting down to business. Find out the prospect's needs at an early stage so that you can tailor your explanation of the benefits of your product or service to those needs. Take a positive "Can do" approach and attempt to resolve any queries and clarify any points that need further explanation. If the prospect raises objections, that may be a sign of interest. Listen carefully, perhaps jotting down what they say so that you can overcome the objections one at a time without missing any.

Avoid revealing all your tactics at once when negotiating

NEGOTIATING SKILLS

Your ability to negotiate comes into play once the customer is interested. The skill is not to lose the order but equally not to give too much away. At this stage you have one important factor in your favour – the buyer obviously wants what you have to offer. Your position is weakened if you have a competitor offering a similar product or service at a better price, but do not be panicked into giving away unnecessary concessions.

Negotiating successfully can be quite good fun. Once you have a fixed bottom price in your mind, all you need to remember is, first, to keep calm and do not let on how keen you are to get the order, and, second, every time the would-be buyer asks for a concession, ask for something in return. When the prospect starts to show a definite interest and is at the stage of

wanting more information, including exactly what the cost will be, introduce your starting price. It should flow naturally in the conversation but, if not, then create the right moment by saying something like: "I know you will want to know the cost, so..." and perhaps taking out your price list at the same time.

The buyer is likely to say that your price is too high. You might defend the price by explaining the high quality of the product or service, or making clear its benefits once more. The buyer may then harden their position by stating what they are prepared to pay. Your starting price should have allowed for a little discounting anyway, and an experienced buyer will presume this. Take your time before replying as your reactions will be carefully assessed. Again defend your price, but offer a reduced price as an introductory offer (or some other scheme which does not create a precedent) and ask for the customer to pay sooner or buy a greater quantity. In other words, you are granting a discount but asking for something in return. Another alternative is to negotiate on non-money issues, so you could reduce your price, but equally offer a shorter guarantee, or omit one of the lesser features.

The best deals are where both buyer and seller feel they have done well – a "win-win" situation. This is not only fair on both parties but is good business, for the buyer is more likely to come back to you, will also act as your ambassador, and neither party will have driven such a hard bargain as to jeopardize the other's business. In all your negotiations, avoid confrontation. As a new small business, it is unlikely to achieve anything.

SALES TO AVOID

Be wary of a buyer if the top price they are prepared to pay is much lower than your stated price. If their price is below the minimum you have in mind, then this is not a good sign. Ask again about what exactly the buyer requires to help you form a better idea of their situation and needs, and maybe gain a clue as to why their offer bid is so low. Also, watch out for the "why don't we just split the difference" offer which, at first glance, may sound fair. Work out if the final figure is in fact still above your bottom price.

Finally, sometimes it is better to lose the sale altogether than to enter into a working relationship with a difficult customer or to get into a deal that makes you no money. Experience has also shown that customers who are difficult to deal with are frequently poor payers too – so be warned and, if you are unhappy or have a bad feeling about the deal, trust your instincts and just walk away.

TECHNIQUES FOR CLOSING A SALE

Learn to sense when a customer is ready to buy. He or she may start to ask detailed questions or talk about methods of payment. Listen carefully to the questions and answer them fully. Then you can attempt to close the sale by, for instance, taking out your order book and asking something like "How many do you want in your first order?" or "On what date would you like your first order delivered?" (then discuss quantities). Another technique is to bypass the Yes/No decision completely by discussing details of the order, getting the customer involved, and then taking out your order book. Once the order has been agreed, ask the buyer to sign a duplicate copy of the order form, which should include the agreed price, terms, and timescales.

MAKING A SALE

Salesman smiles and makes eye contact

1 OPENING THE SALE
The salesman approaches the buyer confidently, gaining his complete attention. He introduces himself clearly and shakes his hand firmly.

Buyer touches chin, revealing thoughtfulness and interest

Salesman explains benefit of products

2 SHOWING THE PRODUCTS
After asking about the buyer's needs, the salesman shows the buyer photographs of the relevant products, pointing out key features and potential benefits.

Tense posture indicates some hostility to the product

Salesman listens carefully to objections

3 MEETING OBJECTIONS
The salesman has captured the buyer's interest in one particular product but the buyer has doubts, which he expresses. The salesman listens, considering his possible responses.

If the customer says they need to think it over or otherwise delay making a decision, then try to leave something like your personal catalogue (marked as such) or samples, which you arrange to collect the next day or the day after. This tactic allows you to see the customer face to face again, which gives you a second opportunity to close the sale. It is much more difficult for the customer to turn you down in person than over the phone.

If the customer is unsure because he or she needs a boss's or colleague's opinion, ask for that person to join your discussions or arrange to come back and see them all – try not to let them decide in your absence. If you need to check on any details or cannot come up with a quotation for something a customer has asked

for on the spot, then you have not yet closed the deal. In many businesses a number of meetings are needed before a deal is finally agreed. Be aware of consumer regulations (see p. 171) that provide for a cooling-off period, in which agreements covered by the regulations can be cancelled by the consumer.

Selling in a Retail Context

Small retail outlets fall into two categories: "convenience shops" (such as a newsagent, corner shop, or chemist), and "specialist shops" (such as a boutique or gift shop). In a convenience shop the customer tends to make most of their purchasing decisions before entering, while in a specialist shop the customer tends to make decisions after entering. That is a simplification, but it emphasizes the differences required in selling technique. In the former case there is less opportunity for selling, as you are primarily responding to the customer's requests; selling can still play a part as you can encourage the customer to buy additional (often complementary) purchases.

In specialist shops, active selling plays a greater role. Here are some suggestions:

■ **GREETING** Acknowledge the presence of a customer soon after they enter the shop, by a nod, smile, and a "Hello" or "Good morning", even if you are dealing with another customer. This makes them feel more at home on unfamiliar territory (especially if they have not visited the

Buyer leans forward, expressing cautious interest

Salesman offers alternative features

Buyer makes sure salesman understands his exact requirements

Salesman listens as he takes down order

4 NEGOTIATING
The salesman overcomes the buyer's doubts, explaining how he can have some features adjusted to meet the buyer's specific needs. He then raises the subject of prices.

5 CLOSING THE SALE
The salesman has got the buyer involved in detailed negotiations. He takes out his order book and starts writing out the order, while discussing the quantities needed.

shop before) and it also tends to hold them until you are free to help them. It is a simple, effective strategy.

■ **FINDING OUT MORE** Let the customer browse for a short time and then approach them. Avoid saying "Can I help you?", as you will probably get the universal reply "No, I'm just looking!", which stops your sales pitch dead in its tracks. Instead, try using a question more related to the situation. For instance, in a clothes shop you might ask what colour the customer is looking for. In a gift shop, you might ask if the customer is after something for himself or herself or for a present. The point of these questions is that they tend to open up a dialogue, which has several advantages: first, it is likely to prevent the customer from rushing around the shop

HELPING THE CUSTOMER
The salesperson has found out that ease of aftercare is important to the shopper, so is giving her a leaflet detailing washing instructions. Meeting the customer's needs ensures that the shopper feels her concerns have been answered, and she can buy the item with confidence.

and disappearing out of the door; second, it allows you to find out what the customer needs, enabling you to offer your goods to match those needs; finally, the customer perceives you as being helpful. Being too pushy can, of course, lose sales.

LAYOUT AND DISPLAYS
The shop layout is important to assist your selling and should be discussed with shopfitters who know about retailing your type of goods (see p. 79). Sales material you should have includes showcards and posters or stickers that

are produced by the suppliers of the stock you are carrying. Suppliers may also provide leaflets to be given away free. Particular thought should be given to point-of-sale displays, since these can contribute significantly to your turnover. Point-of-sale displays usually consist of relatively low-priced and often small products that are either an impulse buy or closely related to what the customer is already buying. The main reason why they work is that the customer already has their purse or wallet in their hand, ready to buy, and may be open to buying something else.

The show window is a crucial factor in selling from a specialist shop; it is the magnet that draws people in as they pass by, very often on an impulse. It should be bright and well-lit, attractive, and all the articles on display should be clearly priced. Displays with a theme, such as a seasonal event, or a common colour, are often eye-catching. Your suppliers may offer free display material that you can use to promote a new product (see also p. 80).

Selling by Telephone

The telephone can be a most useful tool in your sales drive, but to use it effectively requires skill and practice. Telesales are often used to sell expensive one-off items such as conservatories, financial products, and fitted kitchens to the general public. They are also used extensively for selling trade advertising and other general business products and services to businesses. When selling by telephone to the public, there is a very low level of take-up. The success rate for businesses is slightly better, but still relatively low.

The main advantages of selling by phone are that you can contact a large number of people in a relatively short period of time, and you can often get through directly to the decision-maker. The main disadvantages of telesales are that you cannot show your product or other

---

TIPS FOR TELEPHONE SALES

1 Try to keep a smile on your face – it makes your voice sound friendlier.

2 Keep your product or sales information in front of you.

3 Remember the customer will be thinking "What's in this for me?" Stress the benefits of what you are selling.

4 Understanding the customer's needs is half the battle.

5 Since there is nothing in writing, always summarize what has been agreed and later confirm it in writing if necessary.

6 Be polite if rebuffed – never be rude or allow yourself to get angry.

7 At the end of the call, pause, then put the phone down after the other person.

8 Keep a brief record of what is said in all your calls.

---

sales material to the customer, and you cannot accurately gauge their reactions from seeing their face or body language.

As with any sales work, preparation is essential. Know the name of who you are calling and what you are trying to achieve with the call. Handle the phone conversation in very much the same way as you would any sales meeting. In your opening statement, identify yourself and your business and state clearly the purpose of your call. Rehearse this opening statement so that it sounds clear and confident, but do not recite it parrot-fashion. Then concentrate on fact-finding and getting across your sales message. Be prepared to answer numerous questions and to enter into negotiations if the caller is interested. If you are planning to make unsolicited calls to private numbers, there are various legal restrictions and you must not call a phone number that has been registered with the Telephone Preference Service.

Selling by Mail Order

This method of selling allows a small business to have customers located almost anywhere. The first problem is finding those customers. Useful techniques are either to acquire a good-quality mailing list, or to advertise (including on your web site) and hope for a response. You need to carry sufficient stock to meet orders promptly, because customers expect a rapid turnaround. Handling phone orders takes a lot of time, but should be made a pleasant experience for the caller, so do not rush them. Payment should be by credit card or by cheque with order, since giving open credit can create problems even if the sums of money are small. Packaging and distribution costs are high, but customers are resistant to paying much for "post and packing", so the product prices need to carry some of the distribution costs. Mail order succeeds mainly when the products are such that the customer is unable to buy them easily from local shops.

Customer Care

Customer care is about developing a long-term relationship with a customer. It is seeing beyond a single purchase to the customer becoming a regular purchaser. Your customers provide your income and your staff's wages, so they are your lifeblood. This fact should determine your sales aftercare, and be central to your attitude and that of your staff. In addition, in a competitive market, the way you treat your customers can be crucial to keeping them. Customer care is more than being friendly to customers and giving them good deals. It involves being concerned about them and their business problems, and taking steps to make their lives easier and offer solutions. An enthusiastic "Can do" approach is

more appreciated by customers than a sceptical approach – the customer knows best what they want and, if you cannot supply it, another business probably will.

Good communication is important to good customer care. A typical situation to avoid is when a long-standing customer phones in to talk to their usual contact in your company, only to be told that the person has left. This can come as a shock to the customer and could have been avoided by a simple letter or e-mail notifying them of the change. Take time to phone customers at regular intervals to check they are pleased with your product and enquire about their current needs. Listen to their ideas – they can often help you in spotting new trends and gaps in the market.

As in all relationships, there may be ups and downs. If you make a mistake, ensure you rectify it promptly, and, just as importantly, apologize to the appropriate person. If a customer is angry, remain calm and put all your efforts into resolving the cause of their anger.

CREATING A CUSTOMER DATABASE

Preferably from day one, you should create and maintain a database of customer particulars. This should record the obvious details such as contact names, addresses, phone, fax, e-mail, and mobile phone numbers, plus, more interestingly, details of their orders, credit record, and any other relevant information, such as dates of visits and outcomes of any problems. Ideally you will be able to pull up this information on your computer screen when the customer calls, so you can respond to whatever they are requesting with the benefit of background knowledge. There are regulations governing confidentiality that you must observe (see p. 171).

REWARDING CUSTOMERS

The reward that is most beneficial to customers is consistent good care and keeping promises. You might like, in addition, to invite selected buyers, one at a time, to your business premises, assuming they work nearby and your premises are relatively impressive. Alternatively you could invite them to lunch or dinner at a local restaurant. The latter approach has the advantage of you meeting them on neutral territory in a low-key, relaxed situation, which allows them to gain insight into you and your business, and vice versa – do not spoil the occasion by trying to sell them anything.

Many businesses like to offer seasonal presents to their customers. Before doing this, ask yourself if handing over a present makes any real difference to your business relationship with the recipient. Once started, it is difficult to stop, as customers might wonder why they received something one year but not the next. If you decide to give seasonal presents, each

should be effective and appreciated. Ideally presents should carry your business name, be useful and reasonably long-lasting, and should be accompanied by a personalized message. There are tax considerations with gift-giving, so check the implications with your accountant.

DOS AND DON'TS OF CUSTOMER CARE

✓ Do follow up on enquiries.

✓ Do provide quotes or estimates quickly.

✓ Do ensure you can access details of your customer when they call.

✓ Do let a customer know if the work is running late or there is a problem.

✓ Do keep them informed of relevant changes in the personnel of your business.

✗ Don't always leave it to customers to make contact with you.

✗ Don't take regular customers for granted.

✗ Don't leave customers in the dark.

✗ Don't be sharp with customers.

✗ Don't be rude or impatient with customers.

EXPORTING

Businesses start to export for different reasons, but the main one is usually the desire to make the most of a good product or service that is applicable to a wider market than just the home country. Another good reason to try exporting is to spread your risk by widening your customer base. Some companies actively pursue an export policy and produce a business plan with that venture in mind, while other companies slip into exporting on being approached by overseas buyers. Like any other major change to your business, exporting needs market research and careful advance planning.

Exporting can be exciting, providing huge opportunities for even the smallest business. The most likely small businesses to undertake exporting are manufacturers – as long as they have the right products to sell. Exporting is not usually a good move for firms that are having problems selling their products at home, unless there is firm evidence that a new market has a larger demand for that product.

There is much official encouragement to go into exporting, but the proprietor of a small business, especially a new business, cannot afford to be dazzled by government promotion. It is important to ensure before you start that exporting will be profitable for your business, and that the structure of your business can support it. As a small business it may be wise to focus initially on one small export area or country and build from there. You may choose to start by exporting to neighbouring or nearby countries, and it is often a good idea to avoid areas with severe transportation difficulties, at least until the export side of your business becomes more established.

WHO MIGHT CONSIDER EXPORTING?

A small business with a suitable product or service should probably not consider exporting unless it is well established in its home market (making it financially strong enough to set out on this new adventure), or at least one of the proprietors has been in exporting before and already has some of the contacts and necessary experience. Beginning to export is almost the equivalent of starting a new business in terms of the time and cost it can take to set up properly. You will need substantial funds, either from profits or from an injection of new capital, and management needs to have the time available that moving into export demands.

CASE STUDY: Making Initial Exporting Arrangements

FIONA OWNED A successful screen-printing business. After a number of years of trading, she was approached at a national gift trade show by a foreign buyer who placed a significant order. This made Fiona think about exporting, as she felt her firm was now well established at home. She had spoken at some length to this overseas buyer and thought that there was scope to sell more in that particular country. Unfortunately the buyer wanted to secure an exclusive arrangement so Fiona had to consider other territories. She wrote to the overseas buyer confirming her terms and decided to add that the exclusive arrangement would be for an initial period of two years and would depend on the buyer's company placing regular orders and paying on time.

Getting into Exporting

As with any new business venture, the first thing to do is to find out more about the market by doing some market research. There are specialists who can help – speak to your local business development unit or trade association. Also try reading economic reports produced on various regions of the world and tourist guides for the country concerned, to get a better idea of the local culture.

AIMS OF MARKET RESEARCH

One key issue to establish is whether there are any differences between the requirements of the export market and your home market. The differences may be due to cultural, climatic, regulatory, or other reasons, and some can be quite surprising. Other aspects to research are the likely size of the market, the strength of any local competition, the way in which the particular trade operates (there may be a strong trade association that has preferred suppliers), and the established means of distribution in the country or region concerned. Find out, too, the prices of competitors' products so that you can work out if your own prices are likely to be acceptable within that context. Check whether or not you will require an import licence for the destination country, if there are any import duties, and if you will require an export licence from your own country. As when undertaking any market research, keep an open mind and assume nothing.

ADVANTAGES AND DISADVANTAGES OF EXPORTING

ADVANTAGES		DISADVANTAGES	
MARKET SIZE	One of the biggest advantages of exporting is that the potential market is much larger than that of your own country.	HIGH COSTS	Travelling abroad to get orders is expensive in time and money. Shipping goods and agents' fees may also raise your prices.
MARKET MATCH	The product or service you are selling might suit certain overseas markets better than your own country's market.	MARKET MISMATCH	Cultural differences can be such that a successful product or service in your own country might have little appeal elsewhere.
DIVERSIFICATION	Selling in markets beyond your own country provides a possible safeguard against a downturn in your own country's economy.	REGULATIONS	You need to find out about local regulations. There may also be import restrictions or onerous duties.
CURRENCY	Exchange rates can give you an advantage if your currency is weak against that of your customers (or a disadvantage if your currency is strong).	SHIPPING	Speak to a shipping agent at an early stage. Note that the expression "shipping" includes both trucking and air freight.

One of the best and most direct ways in which to obtain information on the potential market is to visit an appropriate trade show in the country concerned. At the show, speak to as many people as you can, make contacts, take notes, observe potential competitors closely (including other exporters from your own country), and obtain copies of any relevant foreign trade publications from which you can have selected articles translated later. Although many people will be more than happy to offer advice and assistance, bear in mind that exhibitors are there to do business and are likely to have time to speak to you only if their stand is quiet.

As part of your research, assess whether your product needs modifying to suit other markets

DOING AN EXPORT BUSINESS PLAN

An export business plan is exactly like any other business plan, except that it is primarily concerned with the exporting intentions of the business. For clarity, the plan should show the export funding and cash flow separately from the main business. In practice, there would be no such separation, unless you were to open a foreign currency account to stabilize your prices. The currency used in your plan and cash flow would be your normal one, as you may be dealing in a number of export currencies. When you start exporting, your accounts should show export sales separately for the tax authorities and for the purposes of your own information.

GETTING STARTED IN EXPORTING

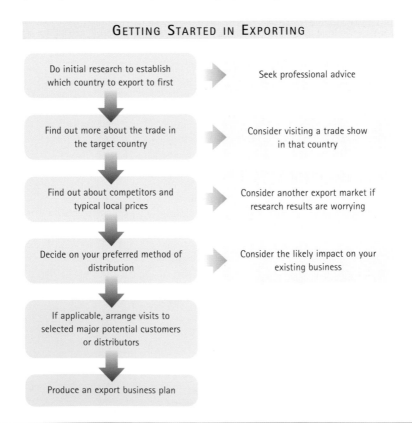

Do initial research to establish which country to export to first

→ Seek professional advice

Find out more about the trade in the target country

→ Consider visiting a trade show in that country

Find out about competitors and typical local prices

→ Consider another export market if research results are worrying

Decide on your preferred method of distribution

→ Consider the likely impact on your existing business

If applicable, arrange visits to selected major potential customers or distributors

Produce an export business plan

MAKING CHANGES AT HOME

If you are going to start exporting seriously, it will have an impact on your existing business. A major factor will be that the proprietor will have to spend a great deal of time setting up the whole export operation. Overseas sales trips take much longer, cost more, and are much more exhausting than taking a sales trip around your own country. Can your business afford to lose a key person for so long, or will it slowly atrophy through neglect? Only you can decide. One option is to take on new staff, either to keep things running at home or to visit the export market. This is a big step, and probably worth considering only once the exporting side of the business is up and running.

DISTRIBUTION

Assuming your market research results are encouraging, you need to consider how best to approach the market.

For a service business, the options depend very much on the type of business concerned; you may have to open a branch office or shop in the country concerned to provide your service. Recruiting and supervising local staff can be a challenge, so franchising might be one solution. Certain types of service business may generate good sales leads via their web sites. Manufacturers have several options:

■ **AGENT** An agent will visit potential customers, take orders on commission (which is typically ten per cent), and then you ship the goods direct to the customers and invoice them individually. You will therefore be responsible for getting payments. Finding a hard-working, reliable agent and controlling customer debt are the main problems. If the agent represents another (non-competitive) business from your country, ask him or her for a reference. Agents often start with enthusiasm, but this can wane if they find that selling your product is going to take some perseverance or they realize they are unlikely to earn much from your sales (being a new, small business).

■ **DISTRIBUTOR** A distributor not only goes out taking orders, but also stocks your goods, so you only need to ship to and invoice them, rather than numerous individual customers. This usually works better than simply having an agent, but the distributor will require a significant discount, and you need to ensure your distributor is reliable and likely to pay you on time. One way to find a distributor is by recommendation through your trade association or other businesses they represent. Do get a credit rating for them, too. As with agents, they should not only sell your goods, but also provide important customer feedback.

■ **DIRECT SALES** To sell directly you can take a stand at a trade show abroad or visit selected customers in person. You may also generate export sales from your web site. In all cases, you would have to ship and invoice each customer individually. Follow-up sales might be difficult or just too expensive for you to undertake, but if you attend the trade shows regularly, your customers will expect to see you there.

■ **COLLABORATIVE PROJECTS** A completely different and often useful approach is a collaboration with an overseas business. This might take the form of providing certain facilities or contacts for them in your country in exchange for the overseas business providing the same services for you.

■ **MANUFACTURE UNDER LICENCE** In this case, an overseas manufacturer agrees to make and sell your product locally. You could supply them with parts, specialized tooling, or even the whole product in kit form. Alternatively, you may just get paid a royalty. This is complex legally, and you will need good professional advice to explore the implications and set up an agreement. It is essential to check out fully the other party's track record, financial status, and integrity.

Sending
Goods Abroad

For most products there are likely to be two main options:

■ **POST** If the goods are lightweight, you may be able to send them by post. This can be by airmail (which is relatively expensive but quick) or surface mail (which is cheaper but takes many weeks to reach most places). The advantages of posting goods are that you have no handling agent's fees, and that there is less onerous paperwork. For small orders, this can be quite useful.

■ **AIR AND SEA FREIGHT** These are effectively the same method as far as efficiency is concerned. A good shipping agent is essential to handle the often complicated documentation associated with air and sea freight, and to advise on the best route and carrier – the most direct way is not always the best. Shipping costs are usually quoted in terms of £/kg (or US $/kg); air is, unsurprisingly, the more expensive. The paperwork must meet the destination country's requirements, or there can be delays and penalties for the importer.

SEA FREIGHT
Goods travel between countries by a variety of methods to keep down costs and maximize efficiency, often being moved from one means of transport to another en route.

PACKAGING

Appropriate packaging is essential as goods that arrive damaged create ill will with customers, take a lot of your time to resolve, and the insurance may not fully cover your financial loss. What constitutes the correct packaging depends on the goods you plan to send, and on what you have agreed with your customers. If the goods are flexible (such as garments), the packaging should flex to absorb ill-treatment, and should be waterproof. If the contents are vulnerable to physical knocks, they need to be isolated by using an inner and outer carton with a gap between the two, and if they are fragile they need an absorption medium in the gap. Generally it is wise to assume that your packages will get rough handling unless you are paying for a premium courier service. Furthermore, warning signs on your packets or cartons such as "Fragile" are universally ignored. Usually, goods on pallets survive better, provided they are kept well within the

TIME SAVER

Packaging can take a large amount of time and money. Try out several standard packaging options to compare the unit cost, ease and speed of use, and weight. When you have found the best method, order the materials in bulk to keep down unit costs.

IMPORTING

This is an entirely different activity to exporting, with its own particular risks and rewards. The main areas a small business is likely to explore are importing stock or raw materials, and arranging for an overseas manufacturer to make your products.

■ **IMPORTING STOCK OR RAW MATERIALS** The main risks are unscrupulous or inefficient suppliers (a common problem is that they substitute when they are out of stock of the item you had asked for), misunderstandings due to language, and unexpected shipping charges.

■ **MANUFACTURING OVERSEAS** Having goods created to your design raises its own particular issues of compliance with your instructions, quality control, and meeting the deadlines you have set.

Ideally, visit the supplier or deal with an agent in your own country. Always discuss with your insurers who should insure the goods while in transit.

pallet edges, but you should ensure that the shipper is equipped to handle the pallet size you plan to use (there are standard sizes). If you are using air freight, the weight of the packaging becomes relevant, and in many cases the sheer cost of the packaging itself can be significant. Experiment with different methods, and take advice from specialist packaging companies.

Getting
Paid on Time

It is one thing to succeed in getting an export order, but it is quite another matter actually to get paid for it. Some countries are known for being particularly good or poor payers in business, although individual companies can differ. For small orders, request payment by credit card or in advance by pro-forma invoice.

For larger orders, as credit card and pro-forma offer no protection for the buyer, request payment by letter of credit or other documentary collection; these are handled by the bank and are relatively safe for both parties, but costly.

If you plan to offer credit, take up references just as you would with any local customer, but do so with even greater attention to detail, and get a credit rating too. Be wary of the customer who places increasingly large orders, always paying on time, but ultimately fails to pay for the last (by now huge) order.

In the event of non-payment, use normal debt collection procedures – issue statements then follow up with a letter, then phone calls, and finally consider visiting the customer abroad if the size of debt warrants it. Some customers assume that because you are far away they can simply ignore you. Arriving in person usually has the desired effect.

STAYING
in business

For your business to survive, you need to have a firm grasp of your financial situation and to know what action to take if things start to go awry. Responding positively to a changing marketplace and formulating your own long-term plan to guide your business will help to keep your venture thriving and on track.

CONTROLLING THE FINANCES

Business is all about money, and the proper management of that money is paramount to the success of any business. This chapter covers the operation of a business bank account, keeping records, how to keep a simple set of accounts, how to do cash-flow management (based on the cash-flow forecast you did for your business plan), minimizing your overheads, solving cash-flow problems, and dealing with late payers.

The first principle to grasp is that it is vital to separate business money from personal money. In a business context this separation is achieved by opening a business bank account and keeping any loose cash from the business in its own container, which can be either a cash till or cash box clearly marked "Business".

Your Business Bank Account

To open a business bank account you will need to see your bank manager. The manager will want to know about the intended business, so take along a copy of your business plan. If you are also looking for finance, leave a copy of your business plan at the bank several days before your appointment, to give the manager time to read it. It is usual, but not essential, to have your business account with the bank that is lending you money. In addition

MONEY SAVER

To avoid bank charges on business cheques, use your business or personal credit card to pay where possible. You can then pay off the business items on your card each month using just one business cheque.

to wanting to know all about you and your proposed venture, and assuming the bank is happy to open an account for your business, the manager will need you to supply information about the following:

■ **NAME OF THE ACCOUNT** If you are setting up a limited company, then the account name is normally the company title in full. If you are going to set up as a sole trader or partnership using the names of the partners, then the account name is usually the name of the proprietor(s) with the words "Business Account" (often abbreviated to "Business A/c") afterwards; for example, "John Smith Business A/c". Where a business name is going to be used for a sole trader or partnership, then the account would usually have the name of proprietor(s) plus the business name; for example, "Joan Smith T/A Simply Perfect".

■ **AUTHORIZED SIGNATORY** If the business is a partnership or there are two or more directors (in the case of a limited company), then the bank will want to know if one signature or more will be necessary on cheques and other authorizations. Some businesses prefer to say that no cheque should be passed without more than one signature, or it may be more practical to instruct the bank not to pass any cheque that is over a specified amount, unless the cheque carries the authorized signatures.

CHOOSING SIGNATORIES
A bank will want to know who in the business will be able to authorize cheques, and whether there are any authorization limits.

■ **STATEMENTS** The bank will also want to know how often you would like to receive a bank statement (monthly is the most usual and is recommended), and to which address the statement should be sent.

■ **DEPOSIT** To open the new account, the bank will normally request a deposit of money from your personal funds.

BANK CHARGES

Whereas you may have enjoyed free banking with your personal account, you will find that business accounts attract charges, and these can add up to a substantial amount over the year. In addition to any loan repayments and overdraft charges, you will usually pay for every cheque you write, every customer's cheque you bank, any cash you withdraw or bank, standing orders and direct debits, and any non-routine services. Shop around at different banks to compare their charges, and ensure you know exactly what you will be paying for. Investigate also whether internet or phone banking will reduce your charges.

KEEPING TRACK OF YOUR ACCOUNT

Once you have opened the business account, it is vital to keep track of the value of the cheques you have written. If your cheque book has stubs, fill them in and then write on the next unused cheque stub the total amount left in the account after deducting the previous cheque. Thus you are always aware of the balance and are never in danger of inadvertently overdrawing

CASE STUDY: Monitoring and Recording Cash flow

JOHN HAD SET up his new shop selling bicycles. He was aware that, although retailing is a cash business, his overheads would be high – how he managed his cash flow would be crucial to his success. He chose a fairly sophisticated cash register that would produce a daily record of sales and VAT for tax purposes and so reduce his accounts paperwork.

It would also give him some management information as to how many of each item or type of item he was selling, which would help with ordering and monitoring stock. John decided he would use computerized accounts from the outset, due to his previous business experience. He also approached his suppliers to try to maximize his credit period for the first 12 months, to help his cash flow.

SINGLE-ENTRY ACCOUNTS BOOK

The example here is for a cash business, and is a record of one week's transactions. In the single-entry system, each transaction is entered only once.

The week's transactions in cash, cheques, postal orders, and credit cards are recorded here

This column records the week's business bank account transactions

In this column is the week's payments made by cash and cheque

The "start of week" figure is 0 for the first ever trading week; then it is the previous week's "end of week" figure

Here, the "start of week" figure is 0 for the first ever trading week; otherwise it is the previous week's "bank balance" figure

Write all daily sales here

This total should equal "cashed cheques" in the next column

Record money from other sources here

It may be easier to record these when your bank statement arrives

Ensure this figure is the same as "total bankings" in the next column

If there is a discrepancy between the balance and the money counted, record it here

Complete this only when your bank statement arrives; the bottom line should equal the balance on the bank statement

Add cheques less bankings that have not yet appeared on the bank statement

Enter this total in the "week's money balance" under "cash payments"

Enter this total in the "week's bank balance" under "cheque payments"

WEEK COMMENCING ....

PAYMENTS RECORD

MONEY RECORD

MONEY IN HAND AT START OF WEEK	£	p
	178	23

DAILY TAKINGS		
Monday	63	12
Tuesday	39	73
Wednesday	127	32
Thursday	98	40
Friday	122	43
Saturday	163	82
Sunday		
TOTAL TAKINGS	614	82

OTHER MONEY, LOANS, ETC		
Cash from bank	50	00
From private a/c	1,000	00
TOTAL	1,050	00

WEEK'S MONEY BALANCE		
Money at start of week plus daily takings plus other money, loans, etc	1,843	05
Less total bankings	1,571	71
Less cash payments	161	02
LEAVES: BALANCE	110	32

MONEY IN HAND AT END OF WEEK	110	22
DISCREPANCY +/-		10

BANK RECORD

BANK BALANCE AT START OF WEEK	£	p
	841	27

DAILY BANKINGS		
Monday	158	23
Tuesday		
Wednesday	80	65
Thursday		
Friday	1,332	83
Saturday		
Sunday		
TOTAL BANKINGS	1,571	71

BANK DIRECT DEBITS, ETC		
Cashed cheques (071)	50	00
Charges/interest	34	75
HP/lease/loan		
TOTAL	84	75

WEEK'S BANK BALANCE		
Bank balance at start of week plus daily bankings less bank direct debits plus bank credits	2,328	23
Less chq payments	1,920	21
LEAVES: BALANCE	408	02

BANK STATEMENT CHECK		
Balance (from above)	408	02
Add total cheques	1,509	00
Less total bankings	1,332	83
LEAVES	584	19

	PAID BY CASH			PAID BY CHEQUE		
	REF	£	p	REF	£	p
Stock/Raw Materials						
A. Jones	133	22	20			
A. Ali & Co				072	87	23
L. Armstrong	134	12	32			
Brown & Son				073	107	24
J. Smith Ltd				076	156	90
Stock/raw materials sub-totals		34	52		351	37
Advertising/promotion						
Business insurances						
Cleaning						
Drawings/salaries/NI/pension (Self)	140	80	00			
Electric/gas/heat (Elec)				074	23	79
Fees (e.g., accountant, lawyer)						
Motor - Fuel				079	9	00
- Repairs/service						
- Tax/insurance						
Postage/parcels	136	1	12			
Rates						
Rent						
Repairs/maintenance						
Staff wages J. Walker				075	22	60
L. Woodall	139	40	00			
Staff PAYE/NI						
Stationery/printing	137	3	50			
Sundries 135 56p 138 £1.32		1	88			
Telephone/fax						
Travelling						
Any other expenses						
Refund customer (by post)				077	13	45
CAPITAL EXPENDITURE						
Van (second-hand)				078	1,500	00
TOTAL CASH AND CHEQUE PAYMENTS		161	02		1,920	21

shown opposite) which comes with instructions. Alternatively, you could buy a blank "analysis book", which is merely ruled with lines and columns, has no headings or instructions (and therefore requires some knowledge of bookkeeping), but has the advantage of being more flexible. The headings used in a standard or a blank book need to relate to what is on tax forms; you can add your own subheadings relating to your own cash management systems if you wish. Cash businesses usually need to keep weekly records, while credit-based businesses usually keep monthly records.

Avoid letting your outgoings exceed your income — you will simply run out of cash

MORE COMPLEX BOOKKEEPING

As your business grows you may need to consider moving to more complex (and expensive) systems. As its name suggests, the double-entry system involves entering each transaction twice – once in the general ledger, and a second time in the appropriate ledger (such as a sales or purchase ledger). Usually the move to a double-entry multi-ledger system occurs not because your turnover has reached any particular level, but because you need more control of purchases and sales made on credit. The double-entry system enables you to keep track of credit transactions to come, as well as the current position. Not surprisingly, operating a multi-ledger system takes much more time and effort and its users usually computerize their accounts. Most computer accounts programs use a double-entry system; before using such a program it is essential to understand the concepts behind it.

PURCHASE AND SALES LEDGERS

A purchase ledger is essential for keeping track of a large volume of goods or services bought on credit. It is simply a lined book with columns to record your purchases from each supplier. Use one page per supplier and title your columns: Order Date; Order Number; Description; Date Goods Received; Date Invoice Received; Debit;

Credit; Balance; and Notes. When, for example, you buy £100 of goods, this is shown in the "Credit" column, and when you pay that supplier the payment is shown in the "Debit" column. Update the purchase ledger at least monthly.

If you are offering credit, you should have a record of who owes you, how much, and how long the bill has been unpaid. This record is called a sales ledger, and complements the purchase ledger. In a sales ledger, the columns would be: Order Date; Customer Order Number; Description; Date Goods Sent; Date Invoice Sent; Debit; Credit; Balance; and Notes. When you sell £150 of goods, for example, this is shown in the "Debit" column, and when the goods are paid for by the customer their

GOOD BOOKKEEPING

1 Always do weekly (or monthly) balances, since these will soon reveal any errors you may have made.

2 A good time to do your books is just after you receive your bank statement.

3 From the bank statement tick off cheques and pay-in stubs against the transactions listed, to reveal any cheques not yet cashed or pay-ins not yet shown.

4 When balancing, if you are out by some amount, then first look for an entry of the same amount that might be in the wrong place or miscounted.

5 If not registered for VAT, your figures should always include any VAT you have been charged.

6 Remember that only expenditure that is wholly and exclusively for your business is normally tax-deductible and therefore worth recording.

7 Keep your bookkeeping up to date – it gets harder to do the longer you leave it.

on a payment, do a revised cash-flow forecast immediately. During especially busy periods, you may need to revise your cash-flow forecast every few days to keep a tight control on required stock levels; this will enable you to keep enough stock to meet demand.

Minimizing Overheads and Expenses

When you start any business, you purchase stock and equipment, maybe rent premises, and perhaps take on staff, all on the not unreasonable assumption that sales will be made, cash will flow in, and these overheads can be sustained. However, if sales are lower than expected you will soon run out of cash. The temptation is to try to increase sales, but the quickest way to solve the problem is to reduce your overheads as they are mostly under your control.

Reduce overheads rather than prices if sales are low

During the many months, or perhaps years, it takes for a business to become established, there is a natural tendency to acquire unnecessary practices and perhaps to have higher overheads than is wise. It is therefore good practice to vet your overheads at least every year, and preferably more often – you will be amazed at how much you can save! This is an essential ongoing process, not just one to follow if your business is in crisis. Analysis of your profit and loss account (see p. 140), comparing the past year with previous ones, can reveal areas worth investigating.

Even relatively small amounts can add up in time. Let us assume your business bank account is being debited £15 each month, for something that you can save on or do without. At first glance you might think it hardly worth the trouble "just to save £15", but over the course of five years (which is no time at all in business terms) this will cost your business a total of £900. Would you willingly give away £900 of your hard-earned profit? There are numerous areas, covered below, where savings are usually possible.

STAFF

Only take on staff when you have to and minimize staffing needs by investing in automation (such as computers). It may be better sometimes to have one high-calibre

USING SPACE WISELY
This shop combines studio space with a selling area. The shelves behind the counter are crammed with pots in progress, while the shop displays finished articles. This efficient use of space keeps overheads to a minimum.

employee who needs less supervision than several of lesser ability. More mature and experienced part-time staff can be particularly worthwhile. Alternatively, try contracting out parts of your work to other companies, or use freelancers. This gives you flexibility to suit a variable workload, but at a higher cost and possibly with less control.

Review work practices regularly, aiming to simplify processes and eliminate unnecessary work. Encourage your staff to suggest ways of improving systems. Try to increase productivity by tight control, comprehensive job descriptions, proper training, and realistic incentives. If you need to make staff redundant, this is a costly and complex business, so seek professional advice first (see p. 176).

MONEY SAVER

If you are trying to save on vehicle overheads, remember that mileage costs money. To minimize the length of journeys, consider using software designed to help you plan your route. This has the bonus of saving valuable time too.

VEHICLES

Choose your purchases carefully, as vehicles represent a major cost and can be more of a liability than an asset. Consider the best way to finance their purchase since there are big differences in costs, especially when maintenance prices are included. Aim to buy nearly new, rather than new, so that someone else takes the initial massive depreciation.

BUSINESS PREMISES

This can be another major overhead, especially in retailing where a prime site is usually vital. In a shop, minimize on-site storage and maximize retail floorspace so that as much space as possible is devoted to selling. In all cases, rent as little space as you can squeeze into. Challenge rent reviews and query rating levels. In time, consider purchasing rather than renting, since the former is usually an investment (if you buy wisely), the latter merely an expense.

HEAT AND LIGHT

We insulate our homes and try to save on domestic energy costs, but seem less interested in doing this in our workplaces, which are often large and poorly insulated, so therefore wasteful. There could be major savings here, especially since the energy market is now highly competitive. Consider consulting a specialist in ways of conserving energy – making a few changes at a reasonable cost could improve energy efficiency and therefore reduce your bills over the long term.

INSURANCES

Check that you are neither under- nor overinsured, and get alternative quotes when your policy comes up for renewal. Major savings can often be made by using an insurer who is used to your particular business (and hence risk) and who can therefore quantify it better than a more general insurer.

PURCHASING

Approve all major purchases yourself. If you decide to delegate some aspects of purchasing, then do so under strict guidelines with definite limits and controls in place. Staff have different priorities to proprietors and this can be reflected in their purchasing decisions.

TRAVEL

If you have to use trains, planes, or hotels, research the different fare or tariff options, since considerable savings are always possible. Ensure your staff do so, too. Investigate deals that offer savings to regular travellers.

FINANCE

If you are borrowing, look at the interest rates you are paying. Investigate the best way to fund your venture. Generally an overdraft is the

cheapest way. Excessive stock levels are one
cause of high borrowings, so check your stock
control. In the long term, aim to be financially
self-sufficient with no need for borrowings.

ADVERTISING AND PROMOTION
Assess if this expenditure is generating
sufficient sales to cover its costs – do not be
surprised if it is not. Advertisements are often
placed in response to salespeople who persuade
proprietors into thinking they must advertise.
Many small businesses will receive a better
response from promotional work rather than
straight advertising.

PHONE BILLS
These are almost always larger than necessary.
Try to reduce the number of long, chatty calls
by using faxes or e-mail. These can
also be transmitted at cheaper
phone times. Investigate alternative
phone companies since this is a
competitive area. Invaluable as the
internet is to businesses, try to
restrict its use to essential work.
As well as running up the phone
bill, it is time taken away from
other tasks.

SUNDRIES
Expenses lumped together under this general
heading, which often includes petty cash
purchases, can cover a multitude of areas,
analysis of which often causes a few surprises
(and further savings).

Solving Cash-flow Problems

Many small businesses are confronted with
cash-flow problems. The term "cash-flow
problem" can cover a variety of ailments, but the
net effect is that the business runs out of money
so that bills cannot be paid. New or recently
started businesses are particularly vulnerable,
with their upfront launch costs and low initial
sales. If the problems are not handled correctly
they might lead to the premature demise of the
venture. In general, cash-flow problems occur
due to either one or, worse, a combination of
the following factors:
■ Overheads too high
■ Sales levels too low
■ Trading levels unexpectedly great
■ Profit margins too small
■ Debtor payments too slow.

DETECTING THE PROBLEM
First of all, you have to be aware that there is a
problem. This may not be so obvious in its
early stages, particularly if accounts are not
fully up to date. One of the best early
indicators is if your cash flow is continually
failing to meet its forecasts. If you
did a "break-even" cash-flow
forecast (where predicted sales
just match outgoings) and then
found that the actual trading
results were falling below these
forecasts, you would know that
the business was heading towards
a major cash-flow problem. For
how to do a cash-flow forecast, see
pp. 54–7, and for cash-flow
management, see pp. 140–42.

Make evolutionary rather than revolutionary changes

In any business, sales go through peaks and
troughs, which may be seasonal in character or
may be signs of something more serious; with a
properly prepared cash-flow forecast, it will be
possible to spot a problem as distinct from the
usual fluctuations. If nothing is done, the
situation will deteriorate and classic warning
signals may become evident. These are:
■ A rising overdraft level (without any specific
reason)
■ Increasing difficulties in paying trade
creditors
■ Falling behind in the monthly PAYE and
National Insurance payments.
These are all very serious signs of impending
disaster and they demand immediate action.

A SURVIVAL STRATEGY

Once a looming cash-flow problem is detected, you must move fast since the business will be growing weaker and there will be less time to make changes and fewer options available.

People tend to react to this situation in two ways, either completely ignoring the problem because they simply cannot face up to it (and they may be unsure what to do) or overreacting and instituting panic measures, which may be ill-considered and potentially damaging. In most people's minds questions fly around. Should they advertise more? Should they cut their prices? Should they sack their staff?

The only sensible course of action is to approach the problem methodically (see the box, right). To do this, you need to work out how to give yourself some time. When a business is not going smoothly the demands on you can increase, making it very difficult to find "thinking time". But if the business is facing a crisis you must simply make time. A practical suggestion is to set aside half an hour before the start of work each day to concentrate your full energy on the problem (since most people are more alert in the morning and the day's dramas have not yet intruded).

LOOKING AGAIN AT OVERHEADS

Reviewing your overhead costs should be a routine task (see pp. 142–4), though the action you choose to take if your business is in difficulty may be more radical than is usual. In some businesses the overheads are simply too high for the level of trading. Possibly the proprietors or directors are drawing too much cash from the business – perhaps forgetting to make provision for tax, VAT, and so on.

TACKLING LOW SALES

Having sales levels that are too low is probably the most common cause of cash-flow problems, especially with new small businesses (under two or three years old), and there are several reasons for this. Many new businesses are set up with a lot of optimism, but insufficient

---

FOUR STEPS TO SOLVING CASH-FLOW PROBLEMS

When business is going badly, it is helpful to have a plan to follow. Try to approach cash-flow problems with a clear mind, concentrating on the crisis at hand, but with an eye on the long term, too.

1 FIND OUT HOW BAD IT IS The problem needs facing up to. Obtain a complete and up-to-date financial picture by quickly putting together a cash-flow forecast, along with lists of all outstanding creditors and debtors, and a further note or list of orders or sales that are likely to materialize over the next few weeks or months.

2 REDUCE YOUR OUTGOINGS The business is running out of cash so the next step is to reduce the outgoings until they match the income. This might require quite drastic action. It may involve reducing staffing levels, getting out of expensive rented premises, and generally cutting back wherever possible.

3 CONSIDER THE OPTIONS Now you know where you are, start to look at the possibilities for improving the situation, and getting the business back on track.

4 TACKLE THE ROOT CAUSE You can now turn your attention to tackling the root cause of the problem. It is important to identify clearly which factor or factors are relevant in your own case – it may be fairly self-evident – and to try and prevent more damage.

---

knowledge of the market and too little capital. Another major factor is that it takes time, often a great deal of time (years, not months), to become established, and this period is normally much longer than most initial business plans allow for. The problem is, of course, that sales during this early period can be lower than that required to support the business (and give you a reasonable wage). Take heart in knowing that there is hardly a business in existence that, at one time or another, has not presented its proprietors or directors with the task of how to increase sales to rectify a cash-flow problem. The first task is to identify the main reason why sales levels are low. A low turnover means that you have too few customers and/or each customer is spending too little. If you are faced with either or both situations, you have a number of options to try:

■ **IMPROVE YOUR SALES AND MARKETING** This is the interface between you and the customer. Making improvements in this area is relatively straightforward and inexpensive, and should be the first option you consider to resolve cash-flow problems. See the box below for details. If all the steps in the selling process are genuinely being done reasonably well (and there is little point in kidding yourself if this is not the case), then the truth may be that there is insufficient demand for your product or service as it currently stands.

■ **MODIFY YOUR BUSINESS** In many cases your analysis of the problem of low sales will reveal a number of areas that need improving, but it may also show that you

REVIEWING SALES AND MARKETING PROCEDURES

Look at all the steps in the selling process in turn to see whether there are any mistakes or omissions you can identify – there are bound to be a few. If any of them are not being done right, this is where to concentrate your efforts.

1 FINDING CUSTOMERS Ask yourself how you expect people to hear about your new business and then try asking some how they actually heard about you. Modify your actions accordingly. Also, work out roughly how many people need to hear about you to produce sufficient enquiries to lead, in turn, to enough sales to support your business.

Many small businesses promote themselves inadequately due to lack of time, money, and possibly expertise. But simply deciding to spend more money on advertising is unlikely to be the right answer and, in any event, your business may not be able to afford much advertising in its present condition. It is better to listen to your existing customers so that you can improve this fertile area. As a simple guide, if your customers are other businesses, then a direct approach by phone or letter followed up by a meeting is likely to give the best results. With the general public, the task is a little more difficult (unless you are a retail business), and the precise approach will require careful thought. For example, if you have a grass-cutting and gardening business, you might put leaflets through letterboxes and then follow up in person. If you have tried this before, you may need to increase the size of your target area or concentrate more effort on higher-income neighbourhoods.

need to modify what you are offering to make it more saleable. Due to your cash-flow predicament there may be a temptation to do something really drastic in terms of changing the product or service on offer, but it is probably much safer to stick to what you are doing, to make a number of fine adjustments, and then to check the response to each of those. These small changes can be implemented much more quickly, at a much lower cost, and involve considerably lower risks than a more radical move. In deciding which changes you could make, think back over the questions, criticisms, suggestions, or shortcomings that have been voiced by would-be customers. Ideally, this is where the inspiration for your modifications should come from initially.

■ **DIVERSIFY** It may be that your initial market research was not quite spot-on, and that the market is really looking for a different product or service, or a major adaptation of what you are currently offering. This is not an unusual situation. However, calm consideration needs to be given to this option, as change or diversification on a large scale must be thought of as akin to an entirely new project, almost like setting up a new venture from scratch. Thus it will take time and money to

---

SALES TECHNIQUE

When reviewing sales techniques, be aware that intrusive or pushy techniques discourage purchasers, who walk away from the sale to avoid being put under pressure to buy.

2 STIMULATING CUSTOMER INTEREST It may be that sufficient customers are aware of you, but their interest has not been caught. Your company or its products or services may not look up-to-date enough, or they may look too upmarket or too downmarket for most of your potential customers. Your leaflet, shop window, or adverts may be confusing to potential customers, or people may simply not realize what you can offer (this is a surprisingly common problem). If you are in retail, try speaking to some of the people who are not making a purchase, perhaps to ask what they are looking for in your shop – their answers could be highly illuminating.

Something else you can do is to look at the competition. What are they doing successfully that you are not? Although your market research investigated competitors, it is useful to look again once you are trading, with the benefit of experience. Also, trading conditions change, and your competitors may have realized this before you.

3 SATISFYING CUSTOMER NEEDS Compare your products or services carefully with those of your competitors. Maybe you include a feature which is putting off potential buyers, or are missing a feature that your competitors are offering, and which makes all the difference. Your business may be projecting one image, but the bulk of your stock may be more suitable for a different image, so you may attract customers but cannot satisfy their needs.

Price is often of crucial importance, so ensure your pricing is correct. Just reducing the price is not necessarily a good idea, since a low price may send the wrong message (that what you are offering is cheap or of low quality). Again, talking to potential customers will shed more light on this.

4 MAKING THE SALE Sometimes the product or service is right, the customer is ready to make the purchase, but the sales technique being used is simply inadequate or even off-putting. Not everyone is a good, natural salesperson and selling does require its own persuasive skills, knowledge, and enthusiasm, even when the product or service is itself excellent. New or refresher courses in sales techniques may be needed.

MAKING TIME FOR REFLECTION

In the first few years of a new business, it is easy to get bogged down in paperwork. For long-term success, it is essential to make time to gain a broader perspective.

Some questions you may have will probably require the assistance of an accountant, such as:
■ How profitable is the business?
■ What is the return on my capital investment? Your annual accounts provide the all-important profit and loss account and a balance sheet. Both may require your accountant to explain the significant aspects of each.

Keeping Up to Date with Developments

The whole world and your own market is constantly changing, and you need to make a major effort just to keep up with events. Look at the checklist opposite to see if you are really keeping up or slipping behind. In running your own business there is a danger that you can become isolated and less aware of changes in the wider world. To overcome this, you need to create a support and information network. This can be formal, such as membership of a trade or small-business organization, or quite informal. In addition, make an effort to keep in touch with former work colleagues.

CHANGE BY EVOLUTION

To survive, almost every business needs to keep evolving. Evolution can be anything from a minor improvement, such as sourcing better paper that does not jam your computer's printer, to a major change, such as the launch of a new product or service. Often small changes added together can make a large positive impact. Your evolutionary changes all have one or more of the following objectives:
■ **INCREASING PROFITS** This is not simply about making more sales, but about making more profit from your present endeavours – which may mean changing your prices, charging for services that you currently offer for free, or changing the balance from low-margin work to higher-margin work.

ASSESSING HOW UP TO DATE YOU ARE

Look at each question and then decide which answer best matches your situation. Score 4 points for each A answer, 2 points for each B, and 0 points for each C. Add up your scores and then look at the score assessments at the bottom.

Do you use the internet?
- A I have a web site.
- B I use the internet for my business.
- C I do not use the internet for my business.

Do you visit trade shows?
- A I visit a relevant trade show at least once a year.
- B I visit a trade show occasionally.
- C I tend not to visit trade shows.

Do you read a trade publication?
- A I subscribe to a trade publication.
- B I occasionally read a trade publication.
- C I don't read any trade publications.

Do you meet others in your industry?
- A I meet others regularly and exchange information.
- B I meet others only on occasion.
- C I rarely meet anyone else in my industry.

Are you a member of your trade association?
- A I am an active member of my trade association.
- B I am a passive member of my trade association.
- C I am not a member of my trade association.

Do you read the financial press?
- A I read several financial publications regularly.
- B I sometimes read a financial publication.
- C I do not read financial publications.

Do you attend seminars or conferences?
- A I usually attend one or two per year.
- B I have attended them on occasion.
- C I do not go to these events.

Are you a member of your chamber of commerce?
- A I am a member of our local chamber of commerce.
- B I am not a member, but occasionally meet members.
- C I am not a member.

Are you aware of changes in relevant laws?
- A I think I am aware of what is coming.
- B I have a hazy idea of what legislation is coming.
- C I do not know what legislation, if any, is in the pipeline.

Do you attend training courses?
- A I attend a training course every year or so.
- B I attend a training course on rare occasions.
- C I do not attend any training courses.

RESULTS

0–10 points
You are probably not keeping up with what is happening in your industry. Set aside time to network and inform yourself.

12–20 points
Although you are keeping up to some extent, there are gaps. Look at the questions where you scored B or C, and improve on these areas.

22–30 points
You are keeping up with many of the developments in your industry, but a little more effort could be beneficial.

32–40 points
You are obviously trying very hard to keep up to date. Well done. Aim to keep your knowledge at the same level, or even higher.

■ **MAKING MORE SALES** No matter how successful you are, you might lose a major customer at any time, so you should always be aware of options for improving sales. Look at ways of increasing your market share, offering new products or services, or moving into other markets, possibly further afield.

■ **MAKING THE BUSINESS RUN MORE SMOOTHLY** Often, the people who start a business are not the best ones to run it. This is partly because they may not be very interested in sorting out administrative matters. However, time spent on these important details helps the business run more efficiently and is good for staff morale and customer confidence.

■ **IMPROVING THE PRODUCT OR SERVICE** Think hard about how you can improve the product you sell or service you offer. The improvements themselves may be modest, but cumulatively they will be significant and the process of continual improvement will keep you ahead of the competition.

■ **REDUCING THE OPERATING COSTS** A winning characteristic of almost every successful entrepreneur is that they are very careful with their money and ensure there is little waste and no unnecessary expenditure. You can learn from them by keeping a tight control on the business finances, especially running costs. This is one activity that should not be readily delegated.

Avoiding Common Pitfalls

Businesses are most vulnerable in their first few years of trading. If you can survive them, your chances of keeping going are much greater and you can consider your business as having become established. One way to help you get through those first tricky years is to learn from the mistakes of others. Look at the checklist on the right to see how well placed you are to avoid various problem areas.

Spare a few minutes to read through this checklist to see how well prepared you are to avoid some of the most common pitfalls of running a business. Give each question some thought and indicate your answers with a tick, cross, or a question mark (if you are unsure). This checklist is intended to provoke thought and suggest aspects of your business, all of equal importance, that you need to look into further; there is no "perfect score" to achieve.

Competitors
Some competitors can be benign, others distinctly less so.
A Do you monitor your main competitors' prices, promotions, expansion, etc? ☐Y ☐N
B Do you subscribe to any trade information source? ☐Y ☐N
C Do you think you are gaining on your competitors? ☑Y ☐N

Suppliers
Your business may be dependent on one or more critical suppliers.
A Do you have a "dual-sourcing" policy or designated alternative suppliers? ☐Y ☐N
B Do you keep in close touch with critical suppliers? ☐Y ☐N

Staff
Your business may be vulnerable if it relies on one or more key staff members.
A Do you have someone to take over should a key worker be ill or leave? ☐Y ☐N
B Are you paying a good wage to discourage staff leaving? ☐Y ☐N
C Do you have an incentive scheme to encourage key staff to stay with you? ☐Y ☐N

Customers
The loss of a major customer or a bad debt could be disastrous.
A Do you have any customer that accounts for more than 25 per cent of your turnover? ☐Y ☐N

CHECKLIST OF PREVENTATIVE MEASURES

B Do you know the potential effects of losing your largest customer? ☐Y ☐N

C Is there any noticeable shift in your customer base or their buying habits? ☐Y ☐N

D Do you have a procedure for checking the creditworthiness of all new credit customers? ☐Y ☐N

E Do you have a procedure for ensuring customers keep within their credit limits? ☐Y ☐N

F Do you have a procedure for chasing late payers? ☐Y ☐N

Financial Control

Lack of financial control is one of the commonest reasons why businesses fail.

A Do you write up your accounts at least weekly? ☐Y ☐N

B Do you do a cash-flow forecast monthly? ☐Y ☐N

C Are you keeping well within any overdraft limit you have? ☐Y ☐N

D Is there a written plan to reduce or end your borrowings? ☐Y ☐N

Pricing

There is a temptation to set a price and stick to it even when things change.

A Have you done a price comparison with rivals in the last six months? ☐Y ☐N

B Are your prices keeping up with inflation? ☐Y ☐N

C Have you changed your prices during the last 12 months? ☐Y ☐N

D Do you know what your profit margin is? ☐Y ☐N

Products

Most products (including services) become dated as time goes on and sales ultimately suffer.

A Are your present "products" in midlife or older? ☐Y ☐N

B Have you new "products" in the pipeline? ☐Y ☐N

C Are these new "products" properly funded and scheduled? ☐Y ☐N

Overheads

Rising running costs can soon overwhelm the profitability of a business.

A Have you reviewed your overheads in the last six months? ☐Y ☐N

B Are your overheads the same or less than last year? ☐Y ☐N

C Do you know which overheads you plan to reduce? ☐Y ☐N

Performance Indicators

It is important to have indicators to give you advance notice of a problem.

A Do you have a business plan that you can follow? ☐Y ☐N

B Do you tabulate or graph key indicators, such as monthly sales? ☐Y ☐N

C Do you analyze your sales to spot significant changes? ☐Y ☐N

D Does your accountant produce an annual profit and loss account for you? ☐Y ☐N

Insurance Cover

A fire, flood, or major theft could wreck your business. Proper insurance cover may cushion the blow.

A In the last 12 months have you reassessed all likely risks? ☐Y ☐N

B Do you have insurance cover for the main insurable risks you have identified? ☐Y ☐N

C Are you complying with all stipulations made by your insurers? ☐Y ☐N

D Do you have any contingency plans, however simple? ☐Y ☐N

E Do you have any procedure to monitor internal or external theft? ☐Y ☐N

RESULTS

If you had a majority of ticks, you are already aware of common pitfalls and taking action to avoid them. If you had more crosses and question marks than ticks, there is still plenty of scope for you to look further at your business and systems to take preventative action.

Two very common reasons for failure are lack of financial controls and insufficient trade (low sales). You should focus most of your attention on avoiding those two key areas. A lack of financial control normally means a business comes to grief because it runs out of cash and is unable to pay its bills. The best way to avoid these cash-flow problems is to practise cash-flow management (see pp. 140–42); this will also identify a situation where there is insufficient trade (which is usually obvious anyway). For suggestions of corrective actions, see pp. 145–8.

LEARNING FROM YOUR MISTAKES

Finally, do not be scared of making the odd mistake. Many successful large companies make mistakes and some of their ventures are disastrous – the difference between them and you is that they can usually afford the mistakes.

If you do make a mistake, large or small, take the time to look at what led up to it, and how you could have acted to avoid it. In this way you will avoid making the same mistake twice, and perhaps learn how to spot when things are going awry earlier and have the time to take some corrective action.

Planning for the Future

Once your business is established and has been trading for a couple of years, it is useful for you to begin to create a long-term business plan. The process may take many months, or even years, while you ponder the different options open to you. As it becomes clear in which direction you should be heading,

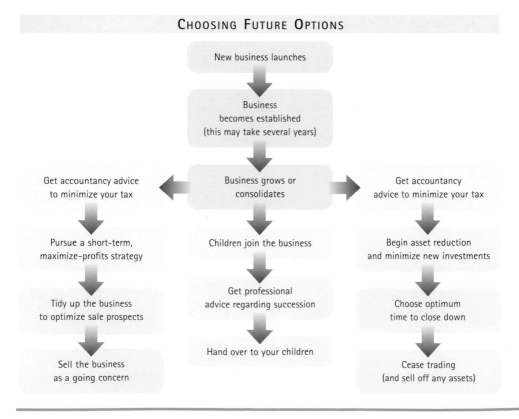

CHOOSING FUTURE OPTIONS

New business launches

Business becomes established (this may take several years)

Business grows or consolidates

Get accountancy advice to minimize your tax

Pursue a short-term, maximize-profits strategy

Tidy up the business to optimize sale prospects

Sell the business as a going concern

Children join the business

Get professional advice regarding succession

Hand over to your children

Get accountancy advice to minimize your tax

Begin asset reduction and minimize new investments

Choose optimum time to close down

Cease trading (and sell off any assets)

then start to structure your thoughts to form the basis of a plan. The format of your plan can be similar to your original business plan, but the objectives are different – the viability of the business is not an issue, and you are not trying to raise finance. What you are aiming to do is to create a five- or ten-year plan with a clear objective. You need to allow for unexpected changes as circumstances change and plans do have a habit of going astray. When you are ready, show the draft to your accountant.

CHOOSING THE WAY FORWARD

Many people assume that a business needs to grow to be considered successful. In fact, many very successful businesses do not grow beyond a certain point, and the people behind those businesses have consciously chosen not to grow their businesses further. There may be many reasons for this, but often it is because the business suits them and is generating sufficient profit for their needs. Instead of striving to grow the business, they will endeavour to consolidate it by making it more efficient and ensuring they keep existing customers and attract sufficient new customers to replace those lost through natural wastage.

Ultimately you may choose to sell or hand on your business, or to cease trading altogether. These options all need long-term planning:

■ **SELLING A BUSINESS** While you are running a business, you minimize your tax by offsetting operating costs against profits to reduce the net profit figure. However, the selling price of a business is a function of its profitability, so it is useful to maximize your profits for the final year (or more) before a possible sale. To do this, first restrict all expenses and, second, as you approach year end, invoice all possible sales. In addition, you should physically tidy up the business and redecorate the premises to make them as attractive as possible.

■ **FAMILY BUSINESS SUCCESSION** This requires specialist professional advice; it is important you bring all family members into the decision-making process at an early stage.

■ **CEASE TRADING** The optimum time to cease trading depends on the nature of the business, the tax position of the proprietors, and many other factors, so this requires good accountancy advice to get the most (tax-paid) money for your business.

PLANNING FOR RETIREMENT

Whatever your age, you need to think about your pension arrangements. The sooner you start, the easier it is to make provision for retirement. The decision has various tax implications and so needs to be discussed with your accountant.

USEFUL information

This section covers the important aspects of the law and tax as they apply to business, providing a straightforward, basic grounding in the numerous and complex regulations that are likely to affect you. The Glossary explains key business terms, while the Useful Contacts and Suggested Reading sections point you towards other sources of information.

LEGAL MATTERS

There are an increasing number of laws and regulations with which businesses, including small businesses, must comply in the UK. This chapter provides general guidance, but should not be regarded as a complete or authoritative statement of the law. For more information, consult a solicitor or the relevant authorities.

Choosing Your Business Status

An early decision you need to make is what legal form your business should take. If you are going to be a one-person business, you could be a sole trader (that is, self-employed) or a limited company. If several people are involved on an equal basis, you need to be a partnership or a limited company. When you start up, inform the Inland Revenue promptly (see p. 177).

SOLE TRADER

This is probably the most common legal status for starting a business. You can trade under

---

DRAWING UP A PARTNERSHIP AGREEMENT

These are suggestions of clauses to consider in a partnership agreement. You may not need all those listed here, and you may wish to include others; this is a starting point:

■ **DESCRIPTION OF THE PROPOSED BUSINESS** This should not limit future developments.

■ **LOCATION** Initial location of the business.

■ **DATE OF COMMENCEMENT** Some agreements also state the duration for which the agreement is to last, though this can be extended by arrangement between partners.

■ **CAPITAL** The initial capital each partner will provide at the commencement. If, due to personal circumstances, the partners contribute different amounts of capital, then they might choose either to: a) apportion the profits in the same ratio as the amounts invested; or b) allow time, say six or 12 months, for the partners to equalize their investments to allow the profits to be shared equally. In both cases voting rights and personal drawings (wages) should be equal.

■ **ROLE OF EACH PARTNER** Definition of the role, adding that the partners will not undertake other employment or self-employment during the period of the agreement. Where one partner is a sleeping partner, this would obviously need to be taken into account.

■ **DECISIONS** The particular circumstances where decisions need to be unanimous to guard against reckless acts by individual partners. For example: agreeing or terminating contracts; offering or terminating employment; entering into or terminating property lease arrangements; lending, borrowing, or removing any property or assets of the business.

■ **VOTING** The voting rights and who might arbitrate should there be disagreement.

■ **OPERATION OF THE BANK ACCOUNT** For example, how many signatures are required on cheques (often only one signature for amounts less than some specified figure).

■ **DIVISION OF PROFITS AND LOSSES** This includes the nomination of an accountant.

■ **LEVEL OF DRAWINGS AND EXPENSES** The latter could have an upper limit per annum.

■ **HOLIDAYS** The length of holidays that can

your own name or a business name. You can also employ staff. Should the business fail, owing money, then you are personally liable, and your creditors can seize your personal possessions through the courts to recover their losses. Many businesses start with sole trader status, but as they grow they usually change to a limited company status for three reasons:

■ It provides limited liability protection of their personal possessions.

■ It is easier for them to raise larger sums of money for expansion.

■ It permits other people to take a stake in the business.

PARTNERSHIP

If two or more people work together and none is an employee of the other(s), then the law regards the arrangement as a partnership. A partnership can take on employees. Unless there is an agreement to the contrary, profits in a partnership have to be shared equally between partners. Likewise, each partner will be regarded by law as "jointly and severally liable" for any debts that the business may run up. What this means in practice is that if the first partner buys a car, for example, using a business cheque that subsequently bounces, the car dealer can pursue the second partner for the entire amount.

It is therefore essential to start off with a good written partnership agreement. Start by drafting your own agreement, get advice from an accountant, and then see a solicitor who can draw up the final document. There are many complex issues involved and you will need professional advice.

be taken. Also, who needs to agree to proposed holiday dates, and any restrictions as to duration or to not taking holidays during prescribed busy times of the year.

■ **ILLNESS OR INCAPACITY** The procedure in the event of illness or incapacity of a partner.

■ **ADMISSION OF A NEW PARTNER** The procedures for admitting a new partner. This might also include a clause that allows the expulsion of one partner under certain specified circumstances.

■ **RETIREMENT OF AN EXISTING PARTNER** Usually the retiring partner is entitled to an equal share of the business assets, excluding goodwill, as valued by the firm's accountants at the date of retirement. The key issue here is that the payment to the retiring partner must be made in instalments that are fair to the outgoing partner and yet affordable by the business. The tax implications for both parties need consideration too. Goodwill should probably be excluded as: a) any goodwill the business has built up has already been enjoyed by the outgoing partner by way of shared profits; b) the departure of the partner might alter any goodwill significantly; and c) it is a very difficult aspect to quantify.

■ **DEATH OF A PARTNER** Usually an agreement will state that the partnership will continue and the estate of the deceased partner will be entitled to a proportion of the business assets, excluding goodwill, with phased payments made to the estate.

■ **TAX CONSIDERATIONS** A clause for tax reasons where the partners (and their executors) elect under the Income and Corporation Taxes Act to have the profits of the business assessed to income tax on a continuation basis as if no change in the partnership had taken place.

■ **DISSOLUTION** The dissolution of the partnership by mutual agreement as to what should happen to the assets.

■ **UNFAIR COMPETITION** It may be wise to incorporate an unfair competition clause if you are concerned that a partner may leave the business at some time in the future and set up in competition with you. The wording can be tricky and must not attempt to prevent a person from earning a livelihood.

GIVING NOTICE

After one month's continuous employment an employee must give at least one week's notice and is generally entitled to the same period of notice from an employer. After two years' employment, an employee is entitled to one week's notice per complete year of service, up to a maximum of 12 weeks' notice for 12 years of service. The employee only needs to give one week's notice unless a longer period has been agreed (and ideally is included in the Written Statement of Employment Particulars).

REDUNDANCY

This occurs when a business wants to reduce its staffing levels, move the business elsewhere, or close down. Redundancy is relevant only if the employee concerned has been with you continuously for two years or more and is aged 20 or over. Such employees may be entitled to a lump-sum redundancy payment, of so many weeks' wage per year of employment, depending on age (there is a maximum weekly pay value used in the calculation). The DTI Employment Service's booklet gives more information. If you plan to make 20 or more employees redundant, you must notify the DTI in advance and enter into a consultation process with your employees or their representatives.

UNFAIR DISMISSAL

Before dismissing anyone, do take professional advice. It is a tricky legal area. Grounds for fair dismissal include incompetence, misconduct, some other substantial reason, or redundancy, but must be both fair and reasonable. In the case of misconduct, unless the employee is found guilty of gross misconduct, such as stealing or assault, it is good management practice to allow the employee adequate opportunity to improve their conduct. They should have had a verbal warning, then at least one (possibly two) written warnings, which should spell out: what they are doing wrong; what they must do to correct their behaviour; the consequences should they ignore the warnings; the fact that the warning constitutes the first formal stage of the disciplinary procedure. The second or final written warning should clearly state that no improvement or any recurrence will lead to dismissal. In addition, you should have fully and fairly investigated the situation, allowed the employee to have their say, and told them how they can appeal.

An employee cannot normally claim unfair dismissal until he or she has worked for you for a year. However, there is no qualifying period if a complaint of unfair dismissal is made due to dismissal for any of the following reasons, all automatically deemed to be unfair: trade union membership; seeking in good faith to assert a statutory employment right; taking certain specified types of action on health and safety grounds; pregnancy; refusing (in certain circumstances) to do shop work on a Sunday; dismissal in relation to the Working Time Regulations or national minimum wage.

After one year's service, a dismissed employee is entitled, at their request, to receive a letter within 14 days explaining why they are being dismissed. A woman dismissed while pregnant or on maternity leave must always receive a letter.

PART-TIME WORKERS
■ **PART-TIME WORKERS (PREVENTION OF LESS FAVOURABLE TREATMENT) REGULATIONS 2000**
Under these regulations, part-timers should: receive the same hourly rate as comparable full-time workers; receive the same hourly rate of overtime as comparable full-time workers, once they have worked more than the normal full-time workers' hours; not be excluded from training simply because they work part-time; have the same entitlements to annual leave and maternity/paternity leave on a pro-rata basis as full-time colleagues. In addition, part-timers who feel they have been treated unfairly by their employer can make a written request for a statement and the employer must reply within 21 days.

FINANCIAL MATTERS

This chapter is an introduction to income tax (and PAYE), National Insurance contributions, corporation tax, capital gains tax, and VAT. The information is for general guidance only and should not be regarded as a complete or authoritative statement on taxation. For more information, consult an accountant, the Inland Revenue, or HM Customs and Excise.

When you start trading, you must notify several tax authorities without delay. If you are a sole trader or starting a partnership, you can now do this using just one form, which will notify your tax office, the Inland Revenue (National Insurance Contributions) Office, and HM Customs and Excise. The form, CWF1 "Notification of Self-Employment", can be found at the back of the booklet CWL1, which is entitled *Starting Your Own Business?* and is available from your local tax office. It can also be downloaded from the Inland Revenue or HM Customs and Excise web sites. The booklet is very readable and provides some useful information on tax.

When you incorporate a limited company, this triggers a response from the Inland Revenue. If you do not hear from them, the onus is on you to notify them. If you are going to draw a salary, this will be subject to PAYE/National Insurance contributions, so you will need a *New Employer's Starter Pack* from the Inland Revenue.

REGISTERING FOR VAT

Although the CWF1 form notifies HM Customs and Excise that you have started in business, it does not actually register you for VAT (Value Added Tax). To register, contact your local HM Customs and Excise office. VAT is a complex tax, but the free booklet *Should I Be Registered for VAT?* is easy and essential reading for any business. It includes a VAT registration application form with notes on how to complete it.

REGISTERING AS AN EMPLOYER

If you are going to employ anyone, you must notify the Inland Revenue so that you can be registered as an employer and operate PAYE (Pay As You Earn). If you are a limited company with salaried directors, you will also have to operate PAYE. Ask your local tax office for a *New Employer's Starter Pack*. As a sole trader or partner (with no employees) you do not operate PAYE.

Income Tax

Broadly speaking, both sole traders and partnerships pay their income tax on their profits via self-assessment. Directors of limited companies pay their income tax by PAYE. PAYE is also the tax system used where there are employees of a business.

INCOME TAX FOR SOLE TRADERS AND PARTNERSHIPS

In the case of sole traders or partnerships, income tax is based on the business profits as declared in the annual self-assessment tax return. The income tax is paid in instalments (currently in January and July each year). In the case of partnerships, the profits of the business are divided equally between the partners unless the partnership agreement says to the contrary. Each partner is liable only for the tax due on his or her share of the partnership's profits.

ACKNOWLEDGMENTS

AUTHOR'S ACKNOWLEDGMENTS

I would like to thank Charlotte Hingston for reading my manuscript and for her many useful suggestions. I would also like to thank my hard-working editors and designer and, finally Julie Servante and Stuart Ramsden for their kind assistance.

PUBLISHER'S ACKNOWLEDGMENTS

Grant Laing Partnership would like to thank the following for their help and participation in producing this book:
Photographer: Mark Hamilton
Proofreader: Nikky Twyman
Indexer: Kay Ollerenshaw
Models: Rhoda Dakar, Augustin Luneau, Katja Mazzei, Francis Ritter, Raffaella Somma.
Thanks also to Blue Island Publishing for kindly allowing us to use their premises.

Dorling Kindersley would like to thank the following for their help and participation in producing this book:
Editorial: Mary Lindsay, Daphne Richardson, Mark Wallace
Design: Sarah Cowley
DTP: Jason Little, Amanda Peers

The illustration on page 103 is used courtesy of amazon.com
The accounts book illustration on page 138 is reproduced with kind permission of Hingston Publishing Co.

PICTURE CREDITS

5 centre and below: gettyone stone; 16: gettyone stone; 23: The Stock Market; 26: Wolfgang Kaehler/Corbis; 36: Richard Olivier/Corbis; 40: gettyone stone; 62: gettyone stone; 63: Robert Harding Picture Library; 64: Paul Thompson/Eye Ubiquitous/Corbis; 68: RW Jones/Corbis; 79: Charles O'Rear/ Corbis; 82–3: gettyone stone; 85: gettyone stone; 88: gettyone stone; 92: Garden Picture Library/Ron Sutherland; 98: gettyone stone; 101: gettyone stone; 110: The Image Bank/ Stephen Derr; 120: gettyone stone; 123: gettyone stone; 132–3: gettyone stone; 135: gettyone stone; 142: gettyone stone; 146: gettyone stone; 148: gettyone stone; 160–61: gettyone stone.

AUTHOR'S BIOGRAPHY

After serving in the RAF, Peter Hingston started his first business in 1979, working with cars near Oxford. He sold this, and later started an electronics manufacturing business in Barbados. Then, with his wife, he launched a fashion shop in Edinburgh, a national trade magazine, and a book publishing business. All traded profitably and were eventually sold, apart from the publishing business, which he runs today. He has written six books on running a small business, some of which have been bestsellers and translated into foreign languages. Peter is also a non-executive director of a large retail business abroad.